D0512418

Modern Slavery

3

...an Slave Child to Middle-Class American

About the authors

Kevin Bales is president of Free the Slaves and advisor to the UN and the US and British governments. He is the author of the award-winning *Disposable People: New Slavery in the Global Economy*, and *Ending Slavery: How We Free Today's Slaves*.

Zoe Trodd teaches in the History and Literature department at Harvard University. Her books include *American Protest Literature* and *To Plead Our Own Cause: Personal Stories by Today's Slaves*.

Alex Kent Williamson of Harvard University is a board-certified pathologist specializing in pediatric and forensic pathology. He is a member of Physicians for Human Rights.

Modern Slavery
The Secret World of
27 Million People

Kevin Bales
Zoe Trodd
Alex Kent Williamson

ONEWORLD
OXFORD

A Oneworld Book

Published by Oneworld Publications 2009

Copyright © Kevin Bales, Zoe Trodd,
and Alex Kent Williamson 2009

The right of Kevin Bales, Zoe Trodd, and
Alex Kent Williamson to be identified as the Authors
of this work has been asserted by them in accordance
with the Copyright, Designs and Patents Act 1988

ISBN 978–1–85168–641–4

Typeset by Jayvee, Trivandrum, India
Cover designedbydavid.co.uk
Printed and bound in Great Britain
by Bell & Bain, Glasgow

Oneworld Publications
185 Banbury Road
Oxford OX2 7AR
England
www.oneworld-publications.com

Contents

Preface
The secret world

There are twenty-seven million slaves alive today. This is more than at any point in history and as many as were seized from Africa in 350 years of the Atlantic slave trade. Put another way, today's slave population is greater than the population of Australia and almost seven times greater than the population of Ireland. These people are paid nothing, are economically exploited, and are under violent control.

They are also invisible. Because slavery is illegal in all countries and banned by international conventions, it has become a hidden crime. Locked away, slaves are difficult to find and count. In the past, when slavery was legally sanctioned in many countries, slaves were counted and measured, their economic value was recorded, and they were listed in legal documents from contracts to wills. For that reason, we have useful, though partial, measures of the numbers, demographics, and economic value of slaves for much of human history. Today the story is much different. Only a small fraction of slaves are reached and freed every year and, until recently, our ignorance of their secret world has been vast. Researchers have therefore faced the problem of data, as well as numerous ethical dilemmas and the sheer controversy – socially and politically – of studying contemporary bondage.

Yet there is a growing recognition of the problem and scope of modern slavery. Scholars have begun to shape a field of research and governments and citizens are awakening to the fact of a new phenomenon: a slavery where slaves are cheap and disposable. Introducing that slavery in all its forms, this book opens up the secret world of twenty-seven million people. Using reliable data, and with an eye for both the history of slavery and the future of abolition, we tackle head-on one of the greatest human rights challenges facing us today.

Chapter one lays out the long history of slavery – from its earliest manifestations in ancient Sumeria, through antebellum American chattel slavery, to twenty-first-century forms around the globe – and discusses abolitionism and slave resistance across the centuries. It introduces modern slavery, including the current situation for slaves in the US and the UK, discusses child slavery, and explains the differences between "Old" and "New" slavery.

Chapter two offers a definition of modern slavery and examines the various forms of slavery today. It discusses the relationship between slavery and human trafficking, the causes of trafficking, and attempts to legislate against it. Chapter three explores the economics of modern slavery, including the role of poverty and government corruption in slavery's growth and persistence, and the predictors of slavery within any one country.

Chapter four focuses on the particularities of the slave experience for women and looks at slavery through the lens of gender. Chapter five explores the dynamics of race, ethnicity, and religion as factors in enslavement, including the practice of hereditary and ritual slavery in some African countries.

Chapter six moves away from racial, religious, and gender identities to examine regional pressures: armed conflict, natural disaster, and environmental destruction. Chapter seven lays out the health risks and consequences of modern slavery, such as HIV infection and post-traumatic stress disorder. Finally, chapter eight offers a blueprint for ending slavery, from government and industry responsibilities to community and individual action.

Throughout we share the stories of individual slaves. Their voices are our truest guide. It is difficult to express the profound gratitude we feel to those many slaves who have overcome bondage and then found the courage to speak out.

This book would also not have been possible without the skill, wisdom, and imagination of Marsha Filion – we couldn't have asked for a better editor. As well, we'd like to thank Dawn Sackett, Fiona Slater, Kate Smith, and all those working with Free the Slaves and Anti-Slavery International, in particular Peggy Callahan. We acknowledge the important anti-slavery work of Judy Hyde and Helen Armstrong; of Lookie Amuzu and Supriya Awasthi; of Marc Levin, and Nekose Wills.

Kevin Bales thanks Humanity United, an independent grant-making organization committed to building a world where modern-day slavery is no longer possible, his son Gabriel Bales, Jolene Smith, Ginny Baumann, Meg Roggensack, Kate Horner, Vithika Yadav, Lookie Amuzu, and Supriya Awasthi, Archbishop Desmond Tutu, and Professor David Richardson, Director of the Wilberforce Institute for the Study of Slavery and Emancipation (WISE) at the University of Hull in England.

Zoe Trodd thanks the Project on Justice, Welfare and Economics at Harvard University's Weatherhead Center, all those at the Australian National University's Humanities Research Centre, in particular Leena Messina, the Andrew W. Mellon Foundation and the American Council of Learned Societies. She also thanks Edward J. Blum, Emma Christopher, Deb Cunningham and all those at Primary Source, Henry Louis Gates, Jr., Lawrence Groo, Brian L. Johnson, Joe Lockard, Timothy Patrick McCarthy, Christine McFadden, Ann Mary Olson, Cassandra Pybus, Leilani Sevilla, Tom Rob Smith, Werner Sollors, Robert Squillace, Michael Stancliff, Chris Stark, John Stauffer, Phyllis Thompson, and Lyn, Geoff, Gabe and Bee Trodd.

Alex Kent Williamson thanks Stephen Geller, Cynthia Nast, Stephen Nichols, Michele Browne, Jill Jarrett, Rob Jenks, Stan Metchev, Kalina Metchev-Simon, Cathy Pagone, Laurie, Greg, Rachel and Daniel Redfern, Anne Simon, Jim Williamson, Drew Williamson and his parents Jon and Sue Williamson.

This book is dedicated to the twenty-seven million.

Kevin Bales, Zoe Trodd, Alex Kent Williamson
Washington, DC, and Cambridge, Massachusetts

Illustrations

1

Perpetual chains: slavery throughout history and today

> Wherever I go ... I'm a slave, chained in perpetual servitude. I may go to your deepest valley, to your highest mountain, I'm still a slave, and the bloodhound may chase me down.
>
> Frederick Douglass, 1845

As the last phrases of the "Declaration of Independence" died away in Rochester's Corinthian Hall on 5 July 1852, the black abolitionist Frederick Douglass rose to speak. He had insisted upon giving his Fourth of July speech, marking American independence, a day late, to remind his white audience that slavery was an anachronism – a rupture in American progress. While acknowledging the Declaration's ideals of liberty and equality, he would protest the long delay in fully realizing them. Sure enough, his speech that day addressed the division between black and white, slave and free, in antebellum America. The nation, Douglass said, is "your nation," its fathers are "your fathers." Then he asked his audience: "What, to the American slave, is your Fourth of July?" It is a cruel sham, he answered. A day of boasted liberties and empty rejoicing that renders slavery "more intolerable."

Today, during bicentennial celebrations of the 1807 and 1808 acts that abolished the British and American external slave trades, Douglass's question rings loud across the years. What, to the modern slave, is the bicentennial? What is the meaning of bicentennial celebrations when slavery still exists – 200 years after those acts, 175 years after the abolition of slavery in the British Empire, and more than 140 years after the American Emancipation Proclamation? And what was the historical journey that brought us to this point, with twenty-seven million people enslaved around the world? Just as Douglass set nineteenth-century slavery in its historical context, pointing to the Declaration of 1776, so we can trace a long pre-history for contemporary forms of slavery.

Slavery throughout history

Long before Douglass himself escaped slavery in 1838, slavery was part of our world. The practice is as old as human history and predates both laws and money. It was part of the Nile cultures from their earliest records; in the First Dynasty, around 7000 BC, slaves were sacrificed in the burials of nobles. Then, in ancient Mesopotamia, drawings in clay from 4000 BC show captives taken in battle by ancient Sumerians, tied, whipped, and forced to work. Sumer's surviving records show a society ruled by a king claiming divine authority over a tightly organized city-state that rested on both serfs and slaves. The records point to wartime raids justified by religion as an important source of slaves.

Slavery continued to thrive in Babylon, a city-state in ancient Mesopotamia and the largest city in the world from 1770 to 1670 BC. Around 1790 BC, the Code of Hammurabi introduced the legal status of a slave. The Code laid out the first complete legal system and reveals the early inter-relationship of religion, law, and slavery in its prologue:

> Bel, the lord of Heaven and earth, who decreed the fate of the land … called by name me, Hammurabi, the exalted prince … so that I should rule over the black-headed people like Shamash, and enlighten the land, to further the well-being of mankind. Hammurabi, the prince, am I … the shepherd of the oppressed and of the slaves.

In this earliest written code of laws the themes of divine approval, conquest, domestication ("shepherd … of the slaves") and slavery are woven together.

The Code outlines a slave system in full operation. There are 282 separate laws regulating most of civil life, and thirty-five of them concern slavery. All are crystal clear: a slave is not a real human being. For example, one of these Babylonian codes explains that if a physician makes a fatal mistake on a patient, his hands are to be cut off – unless the patient is a slave, in which case the physician only has to replace the master's property. Another mandates that if a man strikes a pregnant woman so that she loses her child, the man's own daughter must be killed – unless the woman is a slave, in which case the offender need only pay her master two silver coins.

One of these ancient laws anticipates the United States' infamous Fugitive Slave Act of 1850 (which ordered that any person who helped a fugitive slave to avoid recapture was subject to a fine and imprisonment), instructing that anyone hiding a runaway slave "shall be put to death." And Babylonian slavery shared another major characteristic with American chattel slavery: the free use of violence for control or punishment. The Code of Hammurabi notes that if "a slave strike a free man, his ear shall be cut off," while the Louisiana Slave Code of 1724 explains that a "slave who will have struck his master … will be punished by death."

In Egypt, the period known as the New Kingdom (1570–1070 BC) brought increased military expansion by the Pharaohs and a corresponding explosion of slavery. The most successful military leader of this period, Pharaoh Tutmose, campaigned every year into Syria and Palestine, and claimed to have enslaved more than 100,000 people. Paintings and carvings that survive from this period show ranks of bound captives, from the area that is now Israel and Palestine, and from further south in Africa. The Pharaoh used slave labor for large-scale public works projects, thereby reducing pressure on the peasants and farmers who worked in food production.

As the city-state structure emerged and spread, more societies became hierarchical, militaristic, and slaveholding. Control of farmland and animals was combined with the "domestication" and enslavement of human beings. At their pinnacle, the Greek city-states had large numbers of slaves. Around 400 BC, Athens and its companion port city of Pireaus contained around 60,000 citizens, 25,000 non-citizens, and 70,000 slaves. "With little exception," notes one historian, "there was no activity, productive or unproductive, public or private, pleasant or unpleasant, which was not performed by slaves … in the Greek world." Slaves were seen as essential for the perilous and often deadly work in silver mines that helped to fuel the growth of Athens. About the same time, the work of Plato was building a solid rationalization for slavery based on the inherent inferiority of "barbarians." His pupil Aristotle enlarged this justification, arguing that slavery was good for both slave and master, since each were achieving their true function.

Rome's economy was even more solidly based on slavery and the expansion of the Roman Empire led to a vast slave trade, mainly in captives from foreign conquest and their descendants. But over a period of about seventy years, from 135 BC to 70 BC, the Roman world was rocked by three large-scale slave revolts involving many thousands of slaves. The last of these uprisings, sometimes called the Gladiator War or the War of Spartacus, was initiated by a small band of enslaved gladiators and grew to an army of some 120,000 men that defeated the Roman army several times over a three-year period before being wiped out. Roman laws then became progressively more humane regarding the treatment of slaves in the first century AD. This change reflected an emerging philosophy that held slavery to be against "natural" law. Roman jurists, basing their ideas on the philosophy of the Stoics, suggested that while slavery was universally practiced it was also contrary to nature. With the contraction and fall of the Roman Empire, slavery diminished in proportion to the population held in serfdom.

Between 320 AD and 1453 AD, slavery was a large part of the Byzantine Empire's economy. The expansion by force of the Empire flooded Constantinople with slaves. The emergence of agricultural surplus and ruling elites had established the three main supports of institutionalized slavery: an armed military that could use violence to enslave, a business market for slaves, and a religious elite that provided divine approval for slavery. One element of this approval involved the Judeo-Christian creation myth, namely the Curse of Ham. After the world is washed clean by a great flood, only the family of Noah survives to repopulate the world. Noah's son Ham and his descendents are cursed to be the "servant of servants … unto his brethren," and while the Biblical account makes no mention of skin color, a strong narrative emerged that named Africans as the descendents of Ham. A religious commentary written around 350 AD explains: "[Ham] became a slave, he and his lineage, namely the Egyptians, the Abyssinians, and the Indians."

Slavery also appears in the Jewish Torah, which provides rules for how Jews should treat their slaves. Jews were not supposed to enslave Jews, and if a Jewish person was taken into slavery because of debt, the bondage was limited to six years. But non-Jews could be enslaved for life and their enslavement could be passed on to their children. Around 2100 years ago, however, some Jewish communities began to reject slavery. The Essenes were the first Jewish faith community to outlaw slavery, and the Therapeutae, a Jewish people living near Alexandria, were described by a contemporary in this way: "They do not have slaves to wait upon them as they consider that the ownership of servants is entirely against nature. For nature has borne all men to be free." In fact, practitioners of Zoroastrianism, Hinduism, Judaism, and Confucianism all began to build theologies that were radically different to the past and emphasized compassion and justice.

But the Crusades opened up new Eastern populations to European enslavement. Genoa, Venice, and Verdun became major slave markets, especially after plague decimated the European workforce in the thirteenth century. Slavery became central to the economy of Tuscany. The position of the Church throughout this period was to condemn sales of Christians and to prohibit the buying of any Christians by Jews, while accepting slavery as an institution. Islam promulgated similar rules, forbidding the enslavement of Muslims by Muslims. Then, as the expansion of the European empires into Africa and the Americas began in the fifteenth century, the Church continued its support of slavery in both policy and trade.

Slavery in the British Empire and the United States

Just as the Roman and Byzantine empires had grown on the backs of newly enslaved people, so the Trans-Atlantic Slave Trade marked the beginning of a global Europe. From the 1400s onward, European ships brought captured Africans to Europe as slaves. With the conquest and colonization of the Americas, the trade expanded to include North and South America and became triangular. Ships traveled from Europe to Africa, traded goods for captured Africans, and shipped these African captives to the Americas. The slaves who survived the journey were sold to the colonists, primarily for agricultural work, and the ships were reloaded with tobacco, sugar, cotton, and rum to head back to Europe, where the process would begin again. By 1888, when the Trans-Atlantic Slave Trade finally came to an end with the abolition of slavery in Brazil, between eleven and twenty-eight million people had been taken from Africa.

Many millions of slaves were brought to the North American colonies. Enslaved Africans made up one-fifth of the population of New Amsterdam in 1664, when it was handed over to the British and renamed New York, and by the time of the American Revolution in 1775, the states of Connecticut, Massachusetts, New Jersey and New York held, together, almost 40,000 slaves. And the slave trade did not cease with the American Revolution. Concepts of free religious thought that had emerged in the Protestant Reformation were central to the ideas of equal citizenship and personal freedom in the founding of the new republics of the late eighteenth century. Squaring these beliefs with the powerful economic institution of slavery proved impossible and the result was a series of confused compromises. The constitution of the new United States guaranteed freedom and equality to all citizens, but denied these benefits to slaves. It was a continuing paradox: the first global empires were based on the economic power of slavery yet spread the countervailing ideals of the Enlightenment. Their culmination in the American republic was a revolution for liberty that preserved a slave system.

But as the ideas of the Enlightenment spread, so did a redefinition of slavery. As early as 1769, Adam Ferguson, a Scottish professor of philosophy, argued that "no one is born a slave; because everyone is born with his original rights." Religious bodies began to reject slavery. The first moral tracts against slavery published by Quakers appeared in the early 1700s, and by 1758, Quakers in the American colonies and in Britain had condemned both the slave trade and slaveholding. In 1767 Quaker activists brought a proposed law against slavery into the Massachusetts legislature. The bill failed but the potential for the codification of a human right to freedom was established. Persistent activism by Quakers included the organization of "little associations" against slavery in the American colonies, which laid the groundwork for the debates over slavery that followed the American Revolution.

Then, in 1787, a handful of Quakers and a young Anglican, Thomas Clarkson, formed the Committee for the Abolition of the Slave Trade (re-named the Anti-Slavery Society in 1823). Based in London, it was the world's first human rights organization. Its goal was the complete abolition of the slave trade and the emancipation of the slaves throughout the Empire. Although England itself had few slaves – unlike the Caribbean and the North American colonies – English capitalists were deeply involved in the trade.

By 1791 the Committee had 1300 local branches across Great Britain. The campaign boycotted products produced by slavery, such as sugar from colonies in the Caribbean, raised public awareness, circulated petitions, and lobbied the government to outlaw the slave trade. One lobbyist was the former slave Olaudah Equiano, who published his autobiography in 1789. Here he protested the conditions of the middle passage, explaining that the "closeness of the place, and the heat of the climate, added to the number in the ship … almost suffocated us." Other abolitionists confirmed the realities of Equiano's description by using technical diagrams of this "place" within their print culture. After an abolitionist group in Plymouth produced a diagram of a slave ship, Clarkson and other abolitionists modified it to show the ship loaded with 482 slaves. In 1789, they printed and circulated 7000 posters of the image, which quickly became iconic (see figure 1).

In 1807, the British slave trade was legally abolished. After the end of the Napoleonic wars, the anti-slavery campaign began again, this time aimed at abolishing the institution of slavery itself. Legal slavery in the British Empire ended in 1833. But as one abolitionist movement came to an end, another was just getting started. In the United States, slave importation was legally (if not functionally) ended in 1808, but the US South continued to maintain and grow its slave population by natural increase. Linked to the plantation system and an explosive growth in demand for cotton, the slave population in the southern states of North American grew to about four million by 1860. And as slavery grew in the southern states, so too did American slave resistance.

In 1791, the former Haitian slave Toussaint L'Ouverture had transformed a slave revolt into a revolution, the abolition of slavery, and – eventually – the proclamation of the Haitian Republic in 1804. The success of the Haitian revolution instilled fear into the slaveholders of the southern US and this fear was well founded. By the time of the Civil War, more than 250 small-scale slave revolts had occurred in the South. The most significant of these was Nat Turner's revolt of 1831 in Virginia. Turner led seventy other slaves in a rebellion in Southampton County, Virginia, and the rampage left dead sixty whites and one hundred blacks. It remains the most famous slave revolt in American history.

Beyond this violent slave resistance in the US South itself, Africans also mutinied on slave ships 392 times by 1860 – on as many as ten percent of slave-ship voyages. Most famous were the *Amistad* and *Creole* revolts of 1839 and 1841. In late June 1839, captive West Africans rebelled and seized control of the Spanish slave-ship *Amistad*, which was traveling along the coast of Cuba. The rebel leader was Sengbe Pieh (popularly known as Joseph Cinque) and he ordered the surviving crew members to sail the ship, with its fifty-three slaves, to Africa. But for two months the crew moved the ship back west at night, until it was sighted and seized by the US Navy off the coast of Long Island in late August. The Africans were

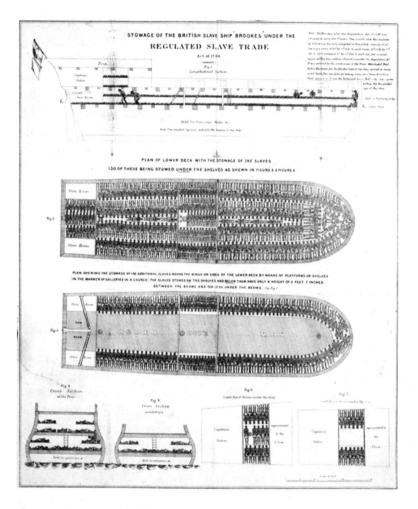

Figure 1 Stowage of the British slave ship Brookes

charged with murder and abolitionists took up their cause. They were declared legally free by a federal trial court in 1840 and by the Supreme Court in 1841. By 1842 they had returned to Africa.

Around the same time, in 1841, Madison Washington led a slave revolt onboard the US brig *Creole* and brought into sharp relief the now divergent paths of Britain and America around the question of slavery. The ship left the port of Richmond, Virginia on 25 October 1841, with 135 slaves. It was bound for New Orleans, Louisiana, where the slaves would be sold at auction. As it neared Abaco Island in the Bahamas, Washington and eighteen other slaves seized pistols and knives, subdued the crew, and sailed for British-controlled Nassau, a port in the Bahamas. The British Emancipation Act of 1833 had ended slavery in the Empire, and the slaves knew they would be freed upon entering the port. The US Secretary of State demanded that the British return the slaves and the ship, but British officials ruled that local laws applied to the *Creole*. The slaves were taken ashore and set free, and the *Creole* eventually reached New Orleans on 2 December 1841, without its human cargo. Such forcible resistance made the anti-slavery crusade a precursor of the violent Civil War.

American abolitionism

Nat Turner and Madison Washington were staging their uprisings in the context of a broader movement for abolition – a crusade that created a new framework for equality and redefined slavery as a moral issue. This redefinition was necessary to combat pro-slavery religious arguments in the nineteenth century. One argument was that Africans would not have had a chance to enjoy the benefits of Christianity, and while enslavement might be harsh it opened a chance to be "saved" and civilized through faith. Another argument hinged on the "curse of Ham" and tried to establish black inferiority on a Biblical foundation. A third argument used carefully selected verses from the Bible that emphasized obedience and order, arguing that God ordained slavery's hierarchy of control.

By the late 1820s, American abolitionism had a manifesto in David Walker's Scripture-infused pamphlet, *Appeal to the Coloured Citizens* (1829). Walker was a free black and most likely a conspirator in Denmark Vesey's plans for slave rebellion in 1822. Like most early abolitionist protest, his pamphlet relied on moral principles rather than economic or political arguments. It encouraged slave uprisings and called for a black revolution. Runaway slaves were allegedly discovered with copies of Walker's *Appeal* in the fall of 1830, and later that year, armed slaves launched an uprising near New Bern, incited by the same pamphlet. Six months later, in August 1831, some observers insisted that Nat Turner himself was prompted to rebellion by Walker's *Appeal*.

While Walker aimed his pamphlet at slaves and free blacks, published slave narratives also changed the opinion of the white American public. Almost from the movement's inception, the major anti-slavery organizations in New York, Boston, and Philadelphia employed dozens of free blacks and former slaves as traveling agents and lecturers to promote the cause. Their published lectures and narratives garnered widespread interest and popularity as soon as they came off the printing presses. Frederick Douglass's 1845 *Narrative* sold 5000 copies in the first four months of publication, and more than 30,000 copies by the beginning of the Civil War. The ten most popular slave narratives sold hundreds of thousands of copies in the US and abroad, went through dozens of editions, and were translated into multiple languages. More effectively than any other genre of abolitionist writing, slave narratives provided readers with intimate, detailed accounts of the brutality of slave life, as well as highlighting the heroism of individual slaves who planned and made their escape from bondage.

Harriet Beecher Stowe, author of the famous anti-slavery novel *Uncle Tom's Cabin* (1852) based many of her characters and scenes on these narratives. In response to the Fugitive Slave Act, passed on 18 September 1850, Stowe had decided to make the nation feel slavery's horrors, and she aimed her sentimental novel, with its cast of fugitives and slaveholders, at northern women in particular. *Uncle Tom's Cabin* had sold 500,000 copies by the end of 1852, eventually selling more copies in the nineteenth century than any book save the Bible. Suddenly "a lady with her pen" had "done more for the cause of freedom ... than any savant, statesman, or politician," as Joshua Giddings exclaimed to Congress in December 1852. And a decade later, Abraham Lincoln purportedly greeted Stowe at the White House with the words: "So you're the little woman who wrote the book that started this great war!"

But by the time of Lincoln's meeting with Stowe, one abolitionist had gone further than the "little woman who wrote the book" and turned rhetoric into action. At midnight on 16 October 1859, the white abolitionist John Brown gave the order: "Men, get on your arms; we will proceed to the Ferry." With his inter-racial band of twenty-one men, Brown launched an attack against the institution of slavery. He captured the town of Harper's Ferry, intending that slaves use arms from its federal arsenal to rise up and claim their freedom. Federal forces overwhelmed the band after thirty-six hours and Brown was indicted on counts of assault, murder, conspiracy, and treason.

Brown's actions, which seemed extreme to moderate abolitionists and much of the watching world, were part of a long-established violent strand in American abolitionism. Alongside the violence of slave revolts, abolitionists advocated violent resistance to slavery. In his *Appeal*, Walker instructed blacks to kill anyone who tried to enslave them, and while Stowe called for empathy in response to the Fugitive Slave Act, numerous black abolitionists advocated a violent response. One, Joshua B. Smith, circulated weapons at an abolitionist meeting, and at another meeting, in Philadelphia on 14 October 1850, several hundred free blacks passed a resolution that they would resist to the death any attempt to enforce the law.

Yet Brown's real power for the abolitionist cause was his combination of words with action. In prison, before his execution on 2 December 1859, Brown swapped sword for pen and converted many to his point of view with letters that were published in newspapers across the North. Derision and vilification became respect and praise. His raid had failed but these letters fueled the passions of northern abolitionists, who turned him into a martyr. In turn, this inflamed passions in the South, where forty percent of the population was black, where black / white ratios on larger plantations exceeded ten to one, and where – consequently – fears of a large-scale slave revolt were acute. Southern leaders used the incident to argue that the South's interests were not represented in federal law. The debate became more and more bitter, Southern politicians charged that their voices were not being heard in

Congress, secession was placed more firmly on the table, and then in 1860, Lincoln was elected when Northern and Southern Democrats splintered into three parties. The chasm forming over slavery had widened beyond the point of no return.

Slavery since American emancipation

The Harper's Ferry Raid, and then Brown's careful packaging of the raid in prison letters, helped to set off a chain of events, and for years commentators would insist that Brown began the war that ended slavery. But what of that end to slavery? Emancipation had not been one of Lincoln's initial war aims; he had sought to save the Union, not destroy slavery. First he tried to convince slaveholders in the border states to gradually eliminate slavery in return for compensation, then eventually came to see that emancipation would weaken the southern economy and so strengthen the war effort.

On 1 January 1863, he signed the "Emancipation Proclamation." The document applied only to states that had seceded from the Union, not the border states or parts of the Confederacy already under northern control, and freedom still depended upon Union victory. Nonetheless, legal ownership of slaves ended in 1865, following northern victory in the Civil War and the thirteenth amendment to the US Constitution, which abolished slavery as a legal institution.

Yet this abolition of legal slavery did not end slavery itself. Now caught in "peonage," a form of debt bondage, thousands of African Americans were re-enslaved by southern planters, who duped or coerced them into signing contracts as sharecroppers. Historian Jacqueline Jones observes that by 1900, "as many as one-third of all sharecropping farmers in Alabama, Mississippi, and Georgia were being held against their will." Farm owners would "hold" the share-croppers' pay, and they were forced to make all their purchases from a "company store," using tickets or orders rather than money. When their annual contracts expired, they found that the crops they raised did not pay the debts they owed. Although it was often apparent that these "debts" were imaginary or impossibly inflated, the penalty for non-payment was jail. Local police helped to enforce this control.

The only alternative was to stay on the land and try to work off the debt, which never seemed to lessen or disappear. Worse, the debt passed from parent to child, binding families to the land with no hope of advancement or escape. The US Congress adopted the "Padrone Statute" in 1874, to combat the practice of kidnapping boys in Italy to be used as street musicians and beggars in American cities, but peonage was practiced across the South and upheld for decades by local and federal governments. A full federal ban was not passed until 1948 and peonage persisted across much of the South well into the 1960s.

Yet even as the US government generally ignored peonage, another form of slavery was very much on the minds of Americans in the first decades of the twentieth century. Large numbers of foreign-born women immigrants were being exploited in the workforce, and some of them were being forced into prostitution – a rapidly expanding practice in the growing industrial cities, and controlled by the same criminal organizations that ran corrupt local governments. Operating from the premise that white women were being lured or abducted, then sold and forced into prostitution by recent immigrants, reformers and religious groups mounted a nationwide campaign. Using the term "white slavery" to describe this systematic sexual exploitation of young women, they waged war against pimps and procurers. The large-scale campaigns that grew out of Christian churches brought together several deep-seated concerns over immigration, changing roles of women, urbanization, corruption, and race. They led to the introduction of legislation for safeguarding endangered white womanhood, including the Mann Act of 1910, which imposed stiff penalties on enslavers of women within US borders. At best, the laws were misguided; at worst they were used as an excuse for ethnic oppression and the wholesale deportation of recent immigrants.

Globally, slavery continued unabated in the twentieth century. Different forms of debt bondage slavery, akin to feudalism, were common throughout India, Pakistan, Nepal, and Bangladesh. The *restavec* system of child slaves in Haiti continued, while in China, the sale of children to be servants accounted for thousands of new slaves each year. In the countries bordering the Sahara Desert, Bedouin tribes such as the Tuareg continued their age-old practice of capturing slaves in sub-Saharan Africa and then selling them in Arab markets in the north. By the first decades of the twentieth century, there were as many as 30,000 slaves in Egypt alone, the majority of them women in domestic servitude. In South America, slaves were used to mine gold and emeralds, grow and harvest sugar, and tap rubber trees in the jungles. And between 1896 and 1915, some 97,000 slaves were shipped from the Portuguese colony of Angola to the islands of Sao Tome and Principe off the west coast of Africa to work on large cocoa plantations run by Europeans.

The twentieth century also saw a vast increase in the amount of state-sponsored slavery. In the Soviet Union some eighteen million people, arrested for their political or religious beliefs, were enslaved in prison camps that operated farms, mines, foundries, and factories from 1930 until the 1960s. And at the height of the Nazi regime, one quarter of Germany's workforce comprised foreign civilians who worked as forced laborers. During the final months of the regime, large numbers of Jewish and other prisoners held in German concentration camps were compelled to work in a range of economic sectors, including munitions and construction. Meanwhile, the Japanese military enslaved as many as 700,000 Koreans, 40,000 Chinese, hundreds of thousands of other Asians, and up to half of the 140,000 Allied prisoners to work under brutal conditions in mines, steel plants, and construction. It also enslaved around 200,000 civilian non-combatant Philippine, Korean, Thai, Vietnamese, and Chinese women and children as forced prostitutes, for use by soldiers. Large "Comfort Stations" that amounted to state-run brothels were established in all the countries occupied by the Japanese military.

Then, after 1945, a population explosion meant an increase in the number of potential slaves. Although there was widespread slavery before World War II, it had tended to be restricted to smaller, and often diminishing, populations. Now the consequent fall in prices of slaves after the population explosion set the stage for a great expansion in global slavery. In the countries where slavery already existed, it increased. In the countries where slavery had died out, it resurged. This was especially true when the Cold War ended in 1989. The collapse of the Iron Curtain that rigidly separated so many countries and the loosening of travel restrictions meant that people and products began to flow across borders in large numbers. Criminals rapidly took advantage of this situation and a revitalized slave trade emerged. In the late twentieth century, slavery evolved into a modern form that devalues individual slaves and increases both their disposability and the profits to be made by the slaveholder.

Abolitionism and anti-slavery legislation in the twentieth century

The last century also saw another great anti-slavery movement unfold: the international effort to end forced labor and slavery in the Congo under King Leopold II of Belgium. King Leopold had established the Congo Free State in 1885 and was running it as a personal business. This business used slave labor to produce rubber, a product in high demand. Whole villages were enslaved to collect rubber in the forests and the death toll during the period of enslavement and exploitation was an estimated ten million people. The English Anti-Slavery Society, which continued its work after the abolition of legal slavery in Britain and the US, took up the cause of slavery in the Congo and presented slideshows of Congo's slaves at more than 600 public events in Europe and the US over the course of two years. In 1908, the Belgian Parliament finally convinced King Leopold to surrender his private state to Belgium, ending slavery in the Congo.

By the time that slavery in the Congo was addressed, two key changes had taken place in how the public viewed slavery. The first change was legal. Slavery became illegal when countries outlawed first the slave trade, then the practice of slavery itself. By the early twentieth century, slavery was illegal across Europe, North America, and South America, with other countries following suit. The second change was that slavery became hidden. Because of its new illegality, slavery moved into the shadows, and there were no longer public auctions of slaves or public documentation of slaveholdings.

With this new form of slavery came new attempts to legislate against it. Rulings in the "Slaughter-House Cases" (1872) ended Mexican peonage, and in the early 1940s the US Supreme Court ruled that employers could not force workers to remain in their jobs nor penalize them for leaving their employment. Internationally, the first agreement abolishing slavery dates to the League of Nations "Slavery Convention" of 1926. The convention defined slavery as "the status or condition of a person over whom any or all of the powers attaching to the right of ownership are exercised." It declared slavery a "crime against humanity" and the slave trader an enemy over whom any state could hold criminal jurisdiction. Some twenty years later, in 1948, the United Nations (UN) passed the "Universal Declaration of Human Rights," which stated: "No one shall be held in slavery or servitude; slavery and the slave trade shall be prohibited in all their forms." It added that "everyone has the right to recognition everywhere as a person before the law." This declaration is signed by every member country of the UN, although not all have ratified it into law. Then in 1956, the UN "Supplementary Convention on Slavery" proscribed "slavery-like" practices, including bondage, serfdom, the forcing or sale of a woman into marriage, and child servitude.

But by the early twentieth century, as legal slavery was fading as a practice, colonial powers had begun imposing mass forced labor on indigenous populations under their control. In response, the International Labour Organisation (ILO) adopted "Convention No. 29" (1930), which outlaws forced labor, defined, with some excep-tions, as "all work or service which is exacted from any person under the menace of any penalty and for which the said person has not offered himself voluntarily." Then, in 1949, the international community adopted the "Geneva Conventions," imposing minimum conditions under which prisoners of war and civilians may be forced to work during times of armed conflict.

That same year saw the first international agreement to prohibit human trafficking: the UN "Convention for the Suppression of Trafficking in Persons and the Exploitation of Others." An amalga-mation of late nineteenth- and early twentieth-century treaties

drafted to address the phenomenon of "white slavery," the convention defined trafficking solely in terms of prostitution, which limited
its ability to combat other forms of human trafficking not linked to
sexual exploitation. The 1979 "International Convention on the
Elimination of Discrimination Against Women" went on to demand
the suppression of "all forms of traffic in women and exploitation of
prostitution of women." Yet no matter how many laws were passed
against it, slavery has never stopped. From the 1990s and into the
twenty-first century, it grew more quickly than our understanding
of its size and reach.

Slavery now

The victory of March 1807 – ending the slave trade in the British
empire – was the first of many abolitionist victories. Legal slavery
in the US ended some sixty years later. But slavery itself didn't
end; making something illegal doesn't make it disappear, it only
disappears from view. Confusing ownership with control, many
people thought that the British legislation of 1807 and 1833, and
the US legislation of 1808 and 1865 meant an end to wholesale
slavery, rather than its legalized form. The laws allowing slavery have
been rescinded, yet slavery occurs on every continent except
Antarctica.

To many people, it comes as a surprise that slavery persists in
the twenty-first century. This modern-day slavery takes various
forms and achieves certain ends but its outcomes are always exploita-
tive in nature: appropriation of labor for productive activities resulting in economic gain, use of the enslaved person as an item of
conspicuous consumption, sexual use of an enslaved person for
pleasure and procreation, and the savings gained when paid servants
or workers are replaced with unpaid and unfree workers. Any particular slave may fulfill one, several, or all of these outcomes for the
slaveholder.

The biggest proportion of the twenty-seven million slaves,
perhaps fifteen to twenty million, is located in South Asia. India is the

world's largest democracy, but within its borders there are at least ten million people trapped in domestic service, forced marriages, forced prostitution, and debt bondage. Most of India's slaves are held in debt bondage slavery and work in brick kilns, rice mills, agriculture, quarries, fireworks production, and garment factories. This slavery persists because of extreme poverty, caste and ethnic discrimination, police corruption, and low arrest and prosecution rates for slaveholders.

Slavery is also concentrated in Southeast Asia, in Northern and Western Africa, and in parts of South America. Some selected hot-spots include Brazil, where laborers are enticed into signing contracts, then taken to remote plantations in the rainforest and forced to burn trees into charcoal at gunpoint; the Dominican Republic, where Haitians are taken across the border and forced to cut cane in sugar plantations; Ghana, where families repent for sins by giving daughters as slaves to fetish priests; Burma, where the military junta enslaves its own people to build infrastructure projects; Sudan, where Arab militias from the North seize Southern Sudanese women and children in slave raids; and Thailand, where women and children are forced into prostitution, for tourists and Thai men.

The ILO estimates that of the total number of slaves alive today, eighty percent are exploited by private agents, and twenty percent are forced to work by the state or rebel military groups. And of the twenty-seven million slaves, most are used in simple, non-technological, traditional work that feeds into local economies. Around the world, a large proportion of slaves work in agriculture. Other common kinds of labor include brick-making, mining and quarrying, textile manufacture, leather-working, gem-working and jewelry-making, cloth and carpet-making, domestic service, forest clearing, and charcoal-making. This forced labor for economic exploitation accounts for approximately ninety percent of slavery in Latin America and the Caribbean, Asia, Africa, and the Middle East, while commercial sexual exploitation accounts for the remaining ten percent. Only in industrialized countries, including the US and Western Europe, does sexual exploitation predominate – accounting for seventy-five percent of slavery.

Child slavery

Whether it involves sexual exploitation, or exploitation in agriculture, industry, and domestic service, a huge proportion of slave labor is performed by children. The ILO estimates that currently there are 8.4 million children engaged in what it calls "the worst forms of labor," defined as debt bondage and serfdom; forced labor, including forced or compulsory recruitment for use in armed conflict; prostitution and the production of pornography; and illicit activities, in particular the production and trafficking of drugs. The figure of 8.4 million breaks down as follows: forced and bonded labor (5.7 million), prostitution and pornography (1.8 million), illicit activities (0.6 million), and armed conflict (0.3 million). Of these children, the majority caught in forced and bonded labor are in the Asia–Pacific region (5.5 million), and in discussing this forced labor, the ILO notes that it involves the presence of one or more of the following elements: a restriction of the freedom to move; a degree of control going beyond the normal exertion of lawful authority; physical or mental violence; and absence of informed consent. Along gender lines, boys tend to be enslaved in commercial farming, petty crimes and the drug trade, while girls are mainly enslaved in commercial sexual exploitation and domestic service.

Within that 8.4 million, around 1.2 million children have been trafficked (transported by force into slavery, whether across international or regional borders). For example, in the United Arab Emirates (UAE), thousands of young boys – some as young as two years old – have been brought from Pakistan, Bangladesh, Sudan, and Mauritania to work as camel jockeys. The UAE enacted a law banning the practice in July 2005, but questions persist as to the effectiveness of the ban. The children are either kidnapped or sold by their families, and are then denied adequate food to ensure that they do not gain weight. And around the world, many children are particularly vulnerable to trafficking and enslavement because they are invisible. A lack of adequate birth registry services in many underdeveloped countries means large numbers of unregistered children. They have little access to schools, social services, and health care, and are easy prey.

But if only 1.2 million have been trafficked, then huge numbers of children – the rest of the 8.4 million – are enslaved without this transportation process. For example, in Haiti, thousands of children termed *restavecs* (meaning "to stay with" in the Creole dialect) are sent each year by their poor rural families to stay with wealthier families. Supposedly they will be sent to school, in exchange for domestic labor. This rarely happens. Instead they work more than fourteen hours a day for no compensation and are frequently abused. Ownership is not asserted, but strict control, enforced by violence, is maintained. The Haitian government estimates that 90,000–120,000 children are enslaved as *restavecs*, but the ILO puts this number at 250,000 and UNICEF at 300,000. Some are as young as four years old, and seventy-five percent are girls, many of whom are sexually exploited.

Child slavery is widespread in some Southern Asian counties as well. There are an estimated 500,000 children trapped in Pakistan's carpet industry, and more than 300,000 children in the same industry in India. Some are lured into bondage by agents' promises to their parents that they will receive good wages, and others are kidnapped. The boys are forced to work for no pay, for up to eighteen hours a day, seven days a week. They are beaten, tortured, branded, kept half fed and half clad, and are usually made to sleep in the loom shed. Cuts and wounds are frequent.

Another hot-spot for child slavery is Ghana's Lake Volta, one of the world's largest lakes. It used to be a source of fish for both the national and export markets, but in the 1960s a dam slowed the vigorous flow of water and destroyed the fishing potential of nearby communities. Facing a newly impoverished environment, some fishermen began to enslave children rather than pay adult workers. With schooling hard to obtain and family incomes around the starvation level, parents will sometimes agree to let their children go in order to gain a 200,000 cedi ($28) "advance" on their child's labor. Normally, the fishermen promise that another 400,000 cedi will be paid to the parents over the next year. The money never comes, and the children work long hours mending, setting, and pulling nets, cleaning and smoking fish, and rowing the fishing boats. Boys as young as six are forced to dive to disentangle nets caught on tree stumps below this man-made lake. The fishermen tie weights to the children to help them descend more quickly. When the water is too cold or the children get caught in the nets below it is not uncommon to find bodies washed up on the shores. While most of the enslaved children are boys, some girls are used for domestic work and to sell the fish in the market. Like other enslaved girls in Ghana, they are likely to be sexually abused.

Modern slavery in the UK and the US

Beyond the developing world, both children and adults are brought into North America and Europe and enslaved. For example, while the full extent of slavery in the UK remains unknown, the best estimates from the government suggest at least 10,000 women and 4000 children have been trafficked into the UK since 1996. In 2003 the Home Office estimated that there were 4000 women in the UK who had been trafficked for sexual exploitation. Most came from Eastern Europe, South-east Asia, Africa, and Brazil. The government has criminalized all forms of trafficking, in the 2004 "Sexual Offences Act" and the 2004 "Immigration and Asylum Act," but the London-based group Anti-Slavery International reports a current lack of protection for those who escape from enslavement in the UK. Many victims continue to be removed as illegal immigrants, with no assessment of the risks to which they may return.

In the US, a conservative estimate is that there are 40,000 people enslaved at any one time and the government estimates that, each year, 14,000–17,500 new people are trafficked into the country, then enslaved through force, fraud, or coercion. They are trapped in slavery for varying lengths of time – most for between two and five years – and they enter the US economy in five main sectors: forced prostitution and sex services, domestic service, agriculture, factory work, and restaurant and hotel work, as shown in table 1. Some victims are born and raised in the US but most are foreign-born. To prevent them from escaping, their captors confiscate their identification documents, forbid them from leaving their workplaces

Table 1 Forms of slave labor in the US

Economic sectors	Percent
Sex services (including exploitation of children)	49
Domestic service	27
Agriculture	10
Factory work	5
Restaurant/hotel work	4
Entertainment	3
Other	2

Source: Free the Slaves and UC Berkeley, 2004

or contacting their families, and threaten them with arrest and deportation.

Of the individuals who are trafficked into the country annually, up to 7000 come from East Asia and the Pacific, up to 5500 from Europe and Eurasia, up to 5500 from South America, up to 700 from Africa, up to 600 from South Asia, and up to 200 from the Near East. Chinese people comprise the largest number of victims, followed by Mexican and Vietnamese people, and traffickers usually recruit victims of their own nationality or ethnic background. Mexico accounts for the majority of federal trafficking cases. The US has strengthened its border patrols in recent years, forcing many migrants from Mexico to rely on underground channels. Smugglers charge exorbitant fees that must be repaid through indentured servitude. But while some victims enter the country illegally, not all are illegal immigrants. Many enter the country legally but because of their poverty or inability to speak English are easily exploited by traffickers.

These operations tend to thrive in states with large populations and sizable immigrant communities, such as California, Florida, New York, and Texas – all of which are transit routes for international travelers. Between 1999 and 2004 alone, the press reported 131 cases of forced labor in the US, involving around 20,000 men, women, and children from a wide range of ethnic and racial groups, and by 2004, forced labor operations had been reported in at least

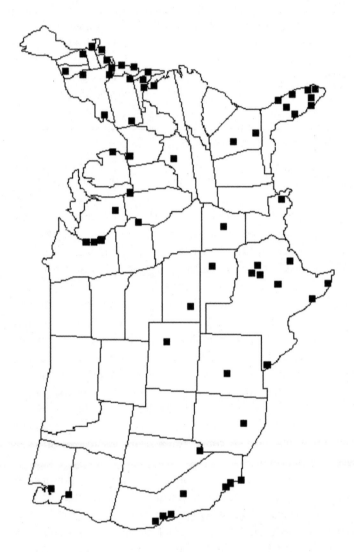

Figure 2 US cities in which instances of slavery have been reported

ninety US cities (see figure 2). We can also identify particular routes into slavery: for example, from China into New York, from Mexico into Texas and Florida, from Thailand into California. Major points of entry include immigration ports such as Los Angeles, New York, and Miami, and victims are then moved around an internal circuit through major cities.

Some 140 years after the "Emancipation Proclamation," slavery continues within the US. Equally persistent is the idea that slavery is over. Most Americans and Europeans have difficulty with notions of contemporary slavery because they confuse slavery with legal slavery. Questions remain: why should we call these practices slavery rather than just another form of superexploitation? Given that legal slavery no longer exists, can we really recognize these people as slaves? How exactly can we define slavery today? Chapter two answers these questions.

2

By yet another name: definitions and forms of modern slavery

> They would not call it slavery, but some other name. Slavery has been fruitful in giving itself names ... and it will call itself by yet another name; and you and I and all of us had better wait and see what new form this old monster will assume, in what new skin this old snake will come forth.
>
> Frederick Douglass, 1865

As modern slaves themselves explain, the fact of slavery is clear: "I was born a slave," explains Salma, who was born into slavery in Mauritania. "Ever since I was old enough to walk, I was forced to work for this family all day, every day." Ramphal, a former quarry slave in India (see figure 3), observes: "When I say I was a slave, or that my parents were slaves, I want you to understand what I'm talking about ... At no time were we free to do what we wanted to do or to make our own choices. That's when we realized we were slaves." But definitions of slavery have caused controversy because opinions differ about which practices should be categorized as slavery and thus designated for elimination.

Since the abolition of legal slavery in the nineteenth century, the word "slavery" has been used for many different things: prostitution, prison labor, low-paid wage labor, segregation. Nearly every culture and historical period has known slavery, and it has been "packaged" differently at each time and place. A dynamic change in packaging occurs, for example, when slavery is legally sanctioned, when that sanction is removed, when different notions of racialization emerge, or when the price of slaves goes up or down. More

Figure 3 Ramphal

than 300 international slavery treaties have been signed since 1815, but none has defined slavery in exactly the same way. Many definitions of slavery have focused on the legal ownership of one person by another, since most slavery in the nineteenth century took that form. Today, there are legal definitions, those given in international treaties and conventions, and those that exist in the public mind. How can we arrive at a definition that encompasses all forms of slavery?

Old versus new slavery

A fascination with the particular form of nineteenth-century chattel slavery hides the larger story of human bondage, in our recent history and our global present. We have to put away the picture that most of us hold in our minds. The history of slavery is seamless. While this history is punctuated by events such as legal abolition, slavery itself has never come to an end. And while different cultures and societies, across different epochs, have imposed the same core elements of violent control and economic exploitation, slavery has

Table 2 Differences between "old" and "new" slavery

Old slavery	New slavery
Slavery not globalized	Slavery globalized
Legal ownership asserted	Illegal and legal ownership avoided
Long-term relationship	Short-term relationship
Racial differences important	Racial differences less important
High purchase cost	Very low purchase cost
Low profits	Very high profits
Shortage of potential slaves	Surplus of potential slaves
Slaves maintained	Slaves disposable

continuously evolved into many forms. Antebellum slavery was just one of these many forms and modern slavery has key characteristics that make it very different. Table 2 shows some key differences between "old" and "new" forms of slavery.

First, modern slavery is globalized, meaning that forms of slavery in different parts of the world are becoming more alike. The way slaves are used and the part they play in the world economy is increasingly similar, wherever they are. Second, while the slave trade of the past was an instrument for the achievement of colony and empire, today's slavery is illegal everywhere and is predominantly the realm of small criminal businessmen. Modern slavery is not a key part of any country's economy. The illegal nature of modern slavery means that legal ownership is rarely asserted over the slave, whereas ownership was clearly demonstrated by bills of sale and titles in the nineteenth-century American South. Third, the length of time that slaves are held has also fallen. In the past, slavery was usually a lifelong condition; today it is often temporary, lasting just a few years or even months. Fourth, slavery is no longer dependent on racial difference.

The remaining four differences all revolve around the new phenomenon of disposable people. Slaves today are cheaper than they have ever been. In the American South before 1860, the demand for slaves was reflected in their price. By 1850, an average field laborer was selling for $1000 to $1800; the equivalent of $20,000 to $40,000 today. But the field-hand slave who cost the equivalent of $40,000 in 1850 costs less than $100 today. Slaves can be acquired in some parts of the world for as little as $10 and the average cost of a human slave around the world is $90. Even given the difficulty of making comparisons between the "true" values of currencies across time, this difference is dramatic, with current prices representing – at most – only .025 percent of the American antebellum rate.

The fact that the cost of slaves has fallen to a historical low means that the balance of supply and demand has been radically changed – today there is a glut of potential slaves on the market. That means they are worth very little but also that they are capable of generating high profits since their ability to work has not fallen with their price. The amount of profit to be made on slaves in Alabama in 1850 averaged around five percent; today profits from slavery start in double figures and range as high as 800 percent. It took twenty years of labor for an antebellum American slave to repay his or her purchase price and maintenance costs; today it takes two years for a bonded laborer in South Asia to do the same.

A fall in price has altered not only the profitability of slavery but also the relationship between slave and master. The expensive slave of the past was a protected investment; today's slave is a cheap and disposable input to low-level production. The slaveholder has little incentive to provide health care or to take care of slaves who are past their prime: while chattel slaves were recognized and treated as sizable investments, today's slaves are disposable. And disposability also contributes to some of the other key differences between old and new slavery. Slaves are so cheap that it is not worth securing permanent ownership. Slavery is short term, because it is not profitable to keep slaves when they are not immediately useful.

Modern slavery defined

The true nature of slavery does not exist in the "packaging" or justifications for slavery. The key to defining it is to look closely at the core characteristics of an enslaved person's life. Across human history, these are the same. Slaves have lost free will, are under violent control, are economically exploited, and are paid nothing. They may be kidnapped or captured, tricked, or born into slavery, and the contextual explanation of why they end up in a state of violent control may be political, racial, religious, mythological, gender-based, ethnic, or combinations of these, but the essence of slavery is controlling people through violence and using them to make money.

It is also important to understand that slavery is not a matter of time. Slavery need not be permanent or life-long. That has never been a requirement, even when slavery was legal. The ancient Babylonian law and the Louisiana Slave Code both allowed for temporary enslavement. For thousands of years people have been captured, snared, coerced, tricked, sold, kidnapped, drugged, arrested, swindled, seduced, raped, or brutalized into slavery, and have then managed to make their way out again through any number of exits. Some were released when their health and strength broke down and they were no longer useful. Sometimes escape took decades and sometimes just weeks, but that did not change the fact that the person had been a slave. The same is true today.

Focusing on the core characteristics of slavery – economic exploitation and the maintenance of violent control – avoids the notion that state-sanctioned or legal slavery is "true" slavery. When considering a situation of extreme exploitation, it is important to ask: "Is this person paid nothing beyond subsistence?" Another important question is: "Can this person walk away, or are they under violent control?" And of all the core characteristics, violent control is the most important: it is the foundation of all slavery. After violent control is established slavery can then take any one of many forms, including debt bondage slavery, contract slavery, slavery linked to religious practices, or state-sponsored forced labor.

The dynamics of slavery do not always involve physical violence: any attempt to escape may be rendered unlikely through threats and psychological coercion (as well as deceit and the confiscation of passports or legal documents). In fact, this psychological manipulation challenges the widely held conception of a slave as someone in chains who would escape if they could. Slaves often know that their enslavement is illegal. Force and psychological coercion have convinced them to accept it, and when they begin to accept their role and identify with their master, constant physical restraint becomes unnecessary. They come to perceive their situation not as a deliberate action taken to harm them, but as part of the normal, if regrettable, scheme of things.

For example, young Thai women held in slavery often find building a relationship with the pimp to be a good survival strategy. Although pimps are thugs, they do not rely solely on violence. They are adept at fostering insecurity and dependence, and cultural norms have prepared these young women for control and compliance. Thai sex roles are clearly defined, and women are expected to be retiring, nonassertive, and obedient – as they are repeatedly reminded. A girl will be told that her parents will suffer if she does not cooperate, that a debt is on her shoulders and must be repaid. So to live in slavery, the young women often redefine their bondage as a duty or a form of penance.

Slavery can therefore be defined as a relationship in which one person is controlled by another through violence, the threat of violence, or psychological coercion, has lost free will and free movement, is exploited economically, and is paid nothing beyond subsistence. Slaves are forced to work for others' profit and are unable to walk away. In some ways this is a narrow definition. It excludes many things that people have called slavery, including sweatshop workers existing on miserly wages. This is not to deny the exploitation that exists in sweatshops or forms of arranged marriage, for example. There is a continuum of exploitation around the world and slavery exists at its extreme end. But if a person is able to walk away – however hard that choice, and however exploited they are – the situation ceases to be slavery.

A clear definition is essential because slavery's variety of forms mean that its underlying nature can be obscured. Both slaveholders and communities that turn a blind eye to slavery have numerous ways to conceal and justify this crime. Religion, "willing" participation, token "payments," the apparent acquiescence in a "contract,"

Table 3 Criteria for defining slavery

Practice ☑–Yes ☒–No	Loss of free will	Appropriation of labor power	Violence or its threat
Debt bondage	☑	☑	☑
Forced labor	☑	☑	☑
Forced prostitution	☑	☑	☑
Caste	☑	☒	☑
Child Abuse	☑	☒	☑
Illegal migrant labor	☑☒	☑☒	☑☒
Organ trafficking	☑☒	☒	☑☒
Prison labor	☑☒	☑☒	☑☒
Prostitution	☒	☑☒	☑☒

or any number of rationalizations can be used as part of the societal or community discourse around the slave/slaveholder relationship. There are families who have been in slavery for generations, and people who were enslaved last week. There are governments that enslave their own citizens, and there is slavery caused by armed conflict. And although each of the manifestations of modern slavery has unique local characteristics, understanding its universal features might enable clear legislation and action. Table 3 therefore tests a range of abuses against the core characteristics of slavery.

Understanding the core attributes that define slavery allows us to consider how these attributes are embedded in a wide variety of forms reflecting cultural, religious, social, political, ethnic, commercial, and psychological influences. The many influences that dictate the form of any particular slave/slaveholder relationship may be unique, but they follow general patterns reflective of the community and society in which that relationship exists. This is part of the challenge of understanding slavery both historically and today – to parse out the underlying attributes shared by all forms of slavery and to analyze and understand the dynamic and various forms slavery can take in individual cases.

The forms of slavery today

Globally, today's slavery is most prevalent in four forms. One form is chattel slavery, the form closest to old slavery, where a person is captured, born, or sold into permanent servitude, and ownership is often asserted. This form is found most often in Northern and Western Africa, and represents a small proportion of slaves in the modern world.

A second form is debt bondage slavery, or bonded labor. The most common form of modern slavery, this is where a person pledges him/herself against a loan of money, but the length and nature of the service is not defined, and their labor does not diminish the original debt. The work of the debtor may ostensibly be applied to the debt, but through false accounting or extortionate interest, repayment is forever out of reach. In many cases of debt bondage the slave's work (and his/her very life) becomes collateral for the debt. The debt passes from husband to wife and from parent to child, and since all the labor power of the debtor is the collateral property of the lender until the debt is repaid, the debtor can never earn enough to repay the debt by his/her own labor.

Debt bondage slavery is most common in South Asia, where there are around ten million bonded laborers in India (though the Bonded Labor Abolition Act of 1976 criminalizes the system), and many thousands more in Nepal and Pakistan. The bondage begins when a crisis occurs, like a serious illness or crop failure. Poor families do not have the resources to buy medicine or enough food. Offered a loan, very often the family knows that they are risking enslavement but accept the offer under unclear terms in order to survive. The debt continually increases because their employer deducts payment for equipment and living expenses, or charges fines for faulty work. If families try to leave, the slaveholder's men retaliate with beatings, rape, and forced eviction. Bonded children are sometimes sold to other contractors, and female workers are frequently raped. They work in brick kilns, rice mills, carpet looms, embroidery factories, and stone quarries. When bonded in these quarries, workers are required to purchase their own materials and are forced to borrow money from the contractors or quarry owners. Children aged four to fourteen are required to work along with their parents for up to fourteen hours a day, carrying loads of rocks in order to maximize production.

A third form is contract slavery. This is the most rapidly growing form of slavery and the second largest form today. It hides behind modern labor relations: contracts guarantee employment, perhaps in a workshop or factory, but when workers arrive, they are enslaved. Contract slavery is most often found in South-east Asia, Brazil, some Arab States, and some parts of the Indian subcontinent.

The fourth form is forced labor. While all slavery is a kind of forced labor, this term specifically means slavery that is practiced not by a person, but by a government or some other "official" group. For example, the country of Uzbekistan in Central Asia sends most of its school and college students into the cotton fields for up to three months each year. The children have no choice and are paid little or nothing for their labor. But the ILO has added two further elements to this definition of forced labor, offering the following typology:

> Forced labor imposed by the State or by armed forces, which includes forced labor exacted by the military or by rebel groups, compulsory participation in public works, and forced prison labor.

> Forced commercial sexual exploitation, which includes women, men and children who have been forced by private agents into prostitution or into other forms of commercial sexual activities.

> Forced labor for economic exploitation, which comprises all forced labor imposed by private agents and enterprises in sectors other than the sex industry. It includes forced labor in agriculture, industry, and services, as well as in some illegal activities.

Within this typology, "forced labor" becomes a synonym for "slavery," and throughout most literature on slavery today, forced labor is used to mean all work or service which is exacted from a person under the menace of penalty and which is undertaken involuntarily.

The ILO has also suggested six indicators of forced labor:

Threats or actual physical harm to the worker;

Restriction of movement and confinement, to the workplace or to a limited area;

Debt bondage, where the worker works to pay off a debt or loan, and is not paid for his or her services. The employer may provide food and accommodation at such inflated prices that the worker cannot escape the debt;

Withholding of wages or excessive wage reductions that violate previously made agreements;

Retention of passports and identity documents, so that the worker cannot leave, or prove his/her identity and status;

Threat of denunciation to the authorities, where the worker is in an irregular immigration status.

In practice these elements are often present in a combination of two or more, and the group Anti-Slavery International argues that just one of these indicators should prompt a thorough investigation, and two or more should identify the situation as forced labor.

There are several other forms that account for a smaller proportion of today's slaves, including ritual slavery (discussed in chapter five). But one common misconception is that another major form exists, called "human trafficking." Trafficking is simply a mechanism or conduit that brings people into slavery. It is one process of enslavement itself, not a condition or result of that process. And it is just a small part of slavery's global picture: there are approximately two and half million people in the world who are in slavery after being trafficked, which is a little under ten percent of all slaves. Most people in slavery are sedentary; they haven't been moved from one place to another. Only in industrialized countries and the Middle East have a significant proportion of slaves been trafficked: approximately seventy-five percent. In Asia, Latin America, and sub-Saharan Africa, trafficked victims account for more than twenty percent of all slaves.

Human trafficking

Nonetheless, trafficking is a global problem. It affects every continent and most countries. As shown in figure 4, Africa is predominantly an origin region for victims of trafficking, and Asia is an origin and destination region. Central and Southeastern Europe is predominantly an origin subregion, and its victims are often exploited in Western Europe. Latin America and the Caribbean represent an origin region, while North America is often a destination for victims trafficked out of Latin America and the Caribbean.

Around 800,000 men, women, and children are trafficked each year across international borders into slavery, and human trafficking is now the third largest source of income for organized crime, after drug smuggling and arms smuggling. Of the 800,000 victims, around eighty percent are female and fifty percent are children. They enter a range of economic sectors, but predominantly the sex industry. A smaller number are subjected to forced labor only, as shown in table 4.

Table 4 International human trafficking data, estimates by various agencies

Variable	US State Department Organization	International Labor	UN Office on Drugs and Crime
Number of trafficking victims	800,000 internationally in 2007	2.45 million internally and internationally between 1995 & 2004	No estimate
Type of exploitation:			
commercial	66%	43%	87%
economic	34%	32%	28%
mixed or other		25%	
Gender and age	80% female	80% female	77% female, 9% male
	50% minors	40% minors	33% minors

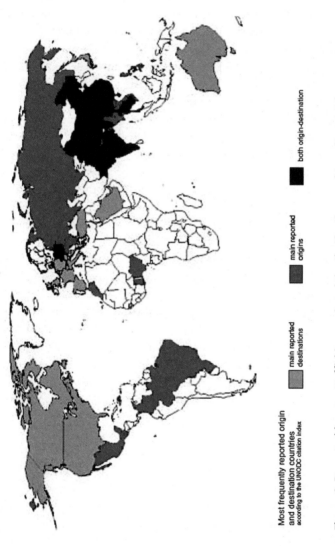

Most frequently reported origin
and destination countries
according to the UNODC citation index

main reported
destinations

main reported
origins

both origin-destination

Figure 4 Reported human trafficking: main origin, destination, and transit countries

But even the figure of 800,000 only represents a small fraction of human trafficking. Beyond the traffic from poorer to richer countries (the poorer global South to the richer global North), today's journey into slavery is made at several other levels: from poorer to richer districts within a country, and from poorer to richer countries within a region. For example, of the estimated 200,000 people who are trafficked into, within, or through India annually, only ten percent of this figure represents cross-border trafficking, while ninety percent is inter-state.

One example of this complex traffic is the movement of enslaved children in West Africa, the key origin region of the trans-Atlantic trade. Here, the flow from the old slave coast is both internal and external (see figure 5). In West and Central Africa alone, up to 200,000 children are trafficked annually. While the poorest children are moved into agricultural work, perhaps from Mali or Burkina Faso into Ghana, Ghanaian children will be sent as domestics into Nigeria or Cameroon, and Nigerian and Cameroonian children will be sent to Europe or North America as domestics or prostitutes. Children are moved constantly from country to country, into various forms of slavery, and to other parts of the world.

Finding a definition for this multi-layered process has been tricky. But in 2000, after several years of negotiation, the UN put forward the "Protocol to Prevent, Suppress and Punish Trafficking in Persons Especially Women and Children." For the first time, the international community had agreed to a definition of trafficking. The Protocol came into force on 25 December 2003, and defines human trafficking in this way:

> The action of recruitment, transportation, transfer, harbouring, or receipt of persons by means of the threat or use of force, coercion, abduction, fraud, deception, abuse of power or vulnerability, or giving payments or benefits to a person in control of the victim for the purposes of exploitation, which includes exploiting the prostitution of others, sexual exploitation, forced labour, slavery or similar practices, and the removal of organs. Consent of the victim is irrelevant where illicit means are established.

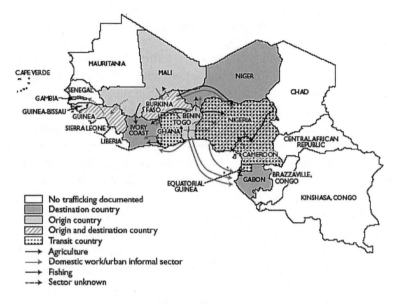

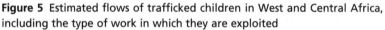

Figure 5 Estimated flows of trafficked children in West and Central Africa, including the type of work in which they are exploited

Trafficking, then, is the crime of carrying someone into slavery by force or fraud, and is a crime whether or not the person agrees to go with the trafficker.

This issue of consent is important because many victims of trafficking begin their journey by consenting to be smuggled from one country to another. While some are kidnapped and transported against their will, numerous others, lured by economic opportunities, pay smugglers to slip them across borders but then find themselves sold to sweatshops and brothels or into domestic service to pay for their passage. The establishment of control occurs after their arrival in the destination country because cooperation is often needed to successfully navigate border crossings and immigration controls. Along the way, their documents are taken away, and the transit house, where they stay at night, is locked. They are fed little, and the "boss" keeps them awake most of the night. Within a few days, sleep deprivation, hunger, and isolation take their toll, and confusion and dependence set in.

Upon arrival in a destination country such as the US, far from family, without any proof of identity, unable to speak the language, hungry, confused, and now threatened, they discover that they are, in fact, slaves. The trafficker may inform them of the large (fraudulent) debts they have incurred in the course of transport and employment recruitment. It is made clear that the debts are large and that the victims must do whatever is asked to clear them. As the level of control increases, the workers will become fully aware of the bad working conditions and lack of freedom they face. They will suffer the threat of violent control that is the hallmark of slavery. They will often be told that the local police will arrest, brutalize, or even kill them if they are found. Force, violence, and psychological coercion are repeatedly used to convince them to accept their situation because, for the trafficker, the aim is a fearful and obedient worker. Then, once under control, the trafficking victims begin their period of enslavement.

Consent at the point of recruitment has led to confusion over the difference between smuggling and trafficking. But by the definition of the UN's "Convention on Transnational Organized Crime," smuggling of migrants is the "procurement of illegal entry into a State of which the person is not a national or a permanent resident to obtain direct or indirect financial or other material benefit." And while many activities of human traffickers (such as using fraudulent travel documents) are also used in smuggling, trafficking goes beyond simply the "procurement of illegal entry into a State." Smuggling and trafficking both involve moving human beings for profit, but in smuggling the relationship between migrants and smugglers usually ends on arrival in the destination country: the criminal's profit is entirely derived from the process of smuggling the migrant. In cases of trafficking, the act of smuggling is just a prelude to and conduit into enslavement. Put another way, human trafficking is smuggling plus coercion or deception at the beginning of the process and enslavement at the end.

In fact, trafficking includes a host of crimes that, again, make it very different to smuggling. The serious crimes committed in the process of trafficking include assault and battery, rape, torture, abduction, sale of human beings, unlawful detention, murder, deprivation of labor rights, and fraud. Yet trafficking is a crime that normally goes unpunished. In the US, for example, around 17,000 people are trafficked into the country and enslaved each year. The country also has 17,000 murders annually. But the national success rate in the US for solving murder cases is about seventy percent. Compare that to the rate for human trafficking. According to the US government's own numbers, the annual percentage of trafficking and slavery cases solved is less than one percent. In 2005, the Department of Justice brought charges against 116 people for human trafficking and slavery, and only forty-five were convicted. In 2006 it only brought charges against 111 people.

This low detection and conviction rate is not due to inadequate legislation, however. In 2000, signaling a new recognition that trafficking is a global problem, President Clinton signed into law the "Victims of Trafficking and Violence Protection Act," also known as the "Trafficking Victims Protection Act" (TVPA). The legislation built upon slavery statutes that were enacted over a century ago. It expanded the definition of forced labor to encompass forms of slavery in the twenty-first century, adding new crimes of human trafficking, sex trafficking, forced labor, and document servitude (withholding or destroying documents as part of the trafficking scheme) to existing sanctions for involuntary servitude, peonage, and slavery. It distinguished smuggling from trafficking, specifying that those who have been trafficked should be recognized as victims of a crime rather than treated as unauthorized migrants, and it broadened the definition of "coercion" to include psychological manipulation.

In terms of punishment, it increased prison terms for slavery violations from ten to twenty years (and life imprisonment if the crime involves murder, kidnapping, or sexual abuse). It required traffickers to pay full restitution to victims and required federal agencies to establish public awareness and information programs about trafficking. And it addressed the question of slavery's aftermath. It enabled survivors to receive housing, psychological counseling, and other social service needs, and it created a new nonimmigrant visa classification. The "T" visa, of which 5000 a year are available, applies to victims of severe forms of human trafficking who are also able to participate in the prosecution of the trafficker. After three years, an individual may adjust to permanent legal resident status. Finally, the TVPA established an Office to Monitor and Combat Trafficking in Persons (or TIP Office). This office is charged with overseeing efforts to end human trafficking abroad, and since 2001 has released an annual "Trafficking in Persons Report." The report outlines anti-trafficking measures worldwide and divides countries into tiers, depending on how rigorously they are combating slavery. Use of diplomacy through the TIP Office has led to new anti-slavery and anti-trafficking laws being passed in a number of countries.

Since the TVPA's passage, however, anti-slavery advocates and service providers have criticized several of its elements. First, it conditions benefits on the cooperation of survivors with federal law enforcement. Though a T visa grants authorization to work, and entitles survivors to receive social service benefits, applicants must document that they are cooperating with law enforcement. This creates the perception that survivors are primarily instruments of law enforcement rather than individuals who are deserving of protection and rehabilitation.

Second, anti-slavery nongovernmental organizations (NGOs) argue that the TVPA needs to include proactive measures for training law enforcement officers and for improving cooperation and information-sharing between federal and state agencies. By and large, victims of forced labor are reluctant to report abuse to law enforcement personnel because they fear retribution from their enslavers. Federal law enforcement personnel are often unable to protect survivors and their families because they lack the necessary legal tools, assistance, and funds to provide a secure and safe refuge. Law enforcement personnel at all levels therefore need training and funding to recognize and assist victims. And, because trafficking is defined almost exclusively as a federal crime to be handled by federal authorities, any coordination between federal and state law enforcement agencies is hindered. This, in turn, has allowed enslavers to go undetected.

The causes of trafficking

But what allowed this new crime to emerge and grow in the first place? A number of factors have led to its expansion, including insufficient penalties against traffickers, the growing deprivation and marginalization of the poor, restrictive migration laws, and lack of information about the realities and dangers of trafficking. Many victims fall prey to trafficking because they are vulnerable to false promises of good jobs and higher wages. As well, in some countries, social or cultural practices contribute – whether the devaluation of women and girls in society or the practice of entrusting poor children to more affluent friends and relatives. Some parents sell their children, or agree to take an "advance" on the wages they will supposedly earn, not just for the money, but also in hope that their children will escape a situation of poverty.

A major factor is easy profits. Criminal groups choose to traffic in persons because it is high-profit and often low risk. Unlike other "commodities," people can be used repeatedly, and trafficking in persons does not require a large capital investment. Profitability is determined by the demand that the "employer" of trafficked persons has for certain skills and attributes in the people they will exploit. These attributes vary according to the jobs or economic sectors in which the "employer" intends to use trafficked persons. The ILO has made estimates of the profits gained from these trafficking victims, and the profits gained from all slaves (see tables 5 and 6).

These estimates show that profits are highest with trafficked victims. The global profits made with the world's slaves who have been trafficked amount to around $32 billion per year (an average of $13,000 per year per slave), while the profits of all slavery amount to around $44 billion per year. Profits are by far the highest in industrial countries, accounting for just under half of the annual profits obtained from trafficking worldwide, and the highest profits are made from forced sexual exploitation (around $28 billion).

We can also look closer at the causes of trafficking to identify the factors that most strongly predict it in a country. The most significant predictors of trafficking from a country, in decreasing order of

Table 5 Annual profits from all slaves

	Total profit in forced commercial sexual exploitation (US$ million)	Total profits in economic exploitation (US$ million)	Global profits (US$ million)
Industrialized Economies	15,388	3,407	18,796
Transition Economies	3,513	145	3,658
Asia and the Pacific	11,190	2,547	13,736
Latin America & Caribbean	2,120	3,554	5,674
Sub-Saharan Africa	565	194	758
MENA	1,125	536	1,661
World	33,902	10,382	44,284

importance, are: the level of a country's governmental corruption; the country's infant mortality rate; the proportion of the population below the age of fourteen; the level of the country's food production; the country's population density; and the amount of conflict and social unrest the country suffers. This means that population pressure and poverty (indicated by infant mortality and food production) are important push factors in trafficking.

Ultimately, then, human traffic is most likely to flow from countries that are poor and suffering from instability and corruption. For example, in the very poorest countries of the world, such as Chad and Mali in Africa, young people are trafficked into domestic service or agriculture in nearby richer countries such as Ivory Coast or Ghana. At the same time, young people from Ivory Coast, Ghana, or Nigeria are tricked and trafficked to even richer countries in Africa, or sent to Europe and North America. Young women from Eastern European countries are tricked by the promise of jobs in

Table 6 Annual profits from all trafficked slaves

	Total profit in forced commercial sexual exploitation (US$ million)	Total profits in economic exploitation (US$ million)	Global profits (US$ million)
Industrialized Economies	13,277	2,235	15,513
Transition Economies	3,283	139	3,422
Asia and the Pacific	9,536	168	9,705
Latin America & Caribbean	572	776	1,348
Sub-Saharan Africa	118	40	158
MENA	1,033	475	1,508
World	27,820	3,834	31,654

North America or Japan and then forced into prostitution upon arrival. The poor of the Philippines and South America are trafficked to Japan or to North America. In large countries such as China or India, children and adults are trafficked from poorer regions to richer regions of the same country, joining trafficking victims who arrive from Nepal or Burma.

We can also identify factors in predicting human trafficking *to* a country. The significant push factors – in decreasing order of importance – are: the proportion of the destination country's male population over age sixty; the level of governmental corruption; low infant mortality; and the level of food production. From a trafficker's point of view the perfect destination country would be a relatively rich country with just enough corruption to allow low risk access across its borders. And sure enough, the almost negligible enforcement of national laws and international conventions against slavery and trafficking in many countries allows slaveholding businesses and brothels to turn immense profits without any tangible threat of prosecution.

But if we can predict human trafficking in this way, can we also predict slavery more broadly? Beyond the factors that have led to an explosion in trafficking, how and why did the other ninety percent of today's slaves – those who were not trafficked – enter bondage? How, over the last few decades, did the world reach a situation where twenty-seven million people are in slavery? Chapter three examines slavery's place in the new global economy.

A money-making system: modern slavery and the global economy

> Money is the measure of morality, and the success or failure of slavery as a money-making system, determines with many whether ... it should be maintained or abolished.
>
> Frederick Douglass, 1857

Today's slaves are disposable people. The price of a slave has fallen to an all-time low, and slaves are now so cheap that they have become cost-effective in many new kinds of work. These disposable people are also a global phenomenon. Slaves from West Africa are found in Paris and New York, slaves from the Philippines are found in Vancouver and Saudi Arabia, and Eastern Europeans, especially women, are dispersed as slaves all around the globe.

In terms of the world economy, slavery is not worth much. Slaves tend to be used in low-value work, such as quarrying and agriculture, and, while slaveholders make a high rate of profit, there may only be five to eight million slaveholders in the world, each holding, on average, a handful of slaves. The ILO's estimate of around $44 billion per year in profits means that slavery is a drop in the large ocean of the global economy. But if slavery is a drop, criminals have become adept at managing its flow. As governments tackle the problem of modern slavery, they are confronting a truly globalized business.

Globalization and the consumer

The most immediate and dramatic impact of globalization has been in the world economy. For centuries countries had controlled the flow of money across their borders, but in the mid-1980s these restrictions ended all at once for most countries. This meant that money could fly around the globe. Hiring or firing workers, buying, selling, or renting factories, investing or diverting funds could all happen with the touch of a button. Businesses could move quickly whenever and wherever they found cheaper labor, and if there was a less expensive factory to rent somewhere else, then a business could just walk away from its current location. As businesses began to spread around the planet, governments had less and less control over their operations; whether the businesses were legal or criminal or a mix of the two.

Throughout history slavery has fluidly adapted to a changing world, and it continues to do so today. As the ILO puts it, slavery and human trafficking are the "underside of globalization." New forms of bondage spread slaves and slave-based activities around the globe with little government control. With the financial systems of globalization, without labor market regulation, slave profits flow smoothly across national borders and governments find it very difficult, if not impossible, to stop the flow of this money. A country's laws stop at its border, but the global slave traffic flows over and under borders like water through a sieve. Many human traffickers operate over the internet, using its global reach to find customers and make deals. And with slavery illegal everywhere, all slaveholders have to act in similarly clandestine ways, hiding their slaves and squeezing out their profits. Locked into a global economy that means that money, goods, and people flow in many directions, slave traffickers increasingly run their "businesses" in similar ways.

Slavery's flows are merging and crossing. In Brazil, slaves are "recruited" in densely populated, economically depressed regions and then shipped over 1000 miles to the forests where they make charcoal. The charcoal, in turn, is shipped another 1000 miles for use in steel mills. The resulting steel is sold to Canada and the US. The European Union imports nearly a million tonnes of Brazilian steel each year to produce everything from cars to buildings to toys. Women are trafficked from Burma or Laos for use in brothels in Thailand, Japan, or Europe. Capital from Hong Kong funds the brothels of Thailand and investment from Europe supports the charcoal operations of Brazil.

While much of today's slave labor is aimed at local sale and consumption, slave-made goods filter throughout the global economy. Millions of slaves in India grow food, quarry stone, or produce other commodities that are used in their own towns and villages, but rugs made by slave children in India, Pakistan, and Nepal are mainly exported to Europe and the US. The phenomenon of globalization means that the goods we buy are increasingly assembled in different parts of the world, using components from all over the world. There are numerous steps and parts that go into making a product and slavery can creep into any one of them.

Slaves are used to produce many of our basic commodities. Originating from numerous different countries, there are documented cases of slavery in our carpets, cocoa, cotton, timber, beef, tomatoes, lettuce, apples and other fruit, shrimp and other fish products, gold, tin, diamonds and other gemstones, shoes, clothing, fireworks, rope, rugs, rice, and bricks. Coffee is sometimes grown with slave labor and some sugar is harvested using slaves. In the Congo, armed gangs force local villagers to dig a mineral called tantalum. The gangs sell the tantalum to exporters who send it to Europe and Asia for use in the production of cell phones and computers. And slavery creeps into investments. Pension funds or mutual funds may have stock in companies that employ other companies that use slave labor.

The problem is even more complex because only a small and hidden proportion of any particular commodity actually has slave input. For example, cotton is grown with slave labor on three continents, but slave-grown cotton is just a tiny fraction of all the cotton grown worldwide. While the American pre-civil war cotton was primarily a slave-made good, the proportion of today's global cotton harvest touched by slaves may be one or two percent at most.

The same problem applies to many other commodities, including chocolate. In Ivory Coast there are about 800,000 farms that grow cocoa – producing about half the world's supply. Young men, normally from poor neighboring countries such as Mali, arrive looking for work. In remote rural areas some are tricked and enslaved into working on the farms. No one knows for certain how many of these farms use slaves, but a good estimate is less than five percent. When the farmers sell their cocoa to wholesalers, the small amount of slave-grown cocoa gets mixed up with the "free" cocoa, and there is no way to tell them apart. The cocoa is exported from Ivory Coast to Europe and North America to be made into chocolate, it is mixed with cocoa from other countries, and it becomes even harder to know what fraction is tainted with slavery.

One attempt to tackle this problem, and remove slave labor from the cocoa supply chain, is the Cocoa Protocol. Established in 2001, it brings together the global chocolate industry, several anti-slavery groups, labor unions, and the ILO. Covering all cocoa-growing regions worldwide, the Protocol serves as a treaty between all the groups and is the first treaty to be struck between an entire industry and the anti-slavery movement. The Protocol established a foundation, the International Cocoa Initiative, which seeks to remove slaves from cocoa production and provide them with a safety net. It received more than $5 million from the chocolate industry between 2002 and 2006, and $4 million for 2007 and 2008. Farm communities are helped to recognize and renounce slave labor, and shelters are ready to care for anyone found in slavery on the farms. Another $1 million was handed over to the ILO to set up the "West African Project Against Abusive Child Labor in Commercial Agriculture," with thirty pilot projects reaching 6000 displaced children in the country. Altogether this is $10 million spent on anti-slavery work by the chocolate industry.

Equally significant was the Protocol's agreement that by 1 July 2005, there would be "credible, mutually-acceptable, voluntary, industry-wide standards of public certification, consistent with federal law" that cocoa was not being grown with child and slave labor. It proposed systems to inspect and certify cocoa at its source. But the certification deadline came and went without result. The system was still being worked out in 2005 and the governments were yet to agree how the inspections could take place. Eighteen months later a pilot program of inspection did begin, but it remained unclear who would pay for it. The local governments wondered why they should have to pay for something forced on them from the outside. Industry was willing to take on some of the cost but saw government responsibility as well. Plus, a number of businesses that use cocoa were not taking part: there is currently no legal requirement for companies to police their supply chain. Work is still being done to find the best way to certify that cocoa is free from slavery.

Prices and population

But how and why did modern slavery even become so embedded in the global economy? The answer begins with slaves' decreased value. Slaves have been expensive capital purchases for all of recorded history. Over the past 4000 years the price of slaves has averaged – as supply ebbed and flowed – between $10,000 and $40,000 in today's currency. But since about 1950, a glut of potential slaves has entered the market and the average price for a human life has plummeted to a historic low of less than $100. The supply of possible slaves is especially plentiful among the billion people who live on about a dollar a day, a population concentrated in the developing world. The fall in price has been so dramatic that the basic economic equation of slavery has been forever altered. Figure 6 shows this dramatic fall in the price of slaves after some 4000 years of high prices. While it is impossible to find a clear equivalent between modern dollars and the currency used in ancient Babylonia or Rome, it is possible to find out how much slaves cost in terms of things that don't change over time. The Price Index in figure 6 reflects a combination of three measures: the value of land, the annual wages paid to a free agricultural worker, and the price of oxen.

   Over the centuries the number of oxen needed to buy a slave never dropped below two. In Sumer in 2000 BC, a slave was worth two oxen. In Greece in 800 BC, a slave was worth four oxen, and in Rome in 200 AD, eight oxen. During the Middle Ages in England a slave was worth between four and eight oxen. In the US between 1847 and 1859, a single slave was worth between four and seven

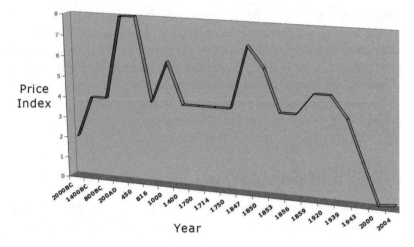

Figure 6 The price of slaves, 2000 bc to 2004 ad

oxen. In a relatively similar context today, that of agricultural debt bondage slavery in Northern India, the acquisition cost of a person is less than one-fifth the cost of a single ox. In land equivalent, the cost of slaves in the past never fell below one productive field, while today the acquisition cost of a slave in India is around one percent of the cost of a single productive field that can be operated by an individual. And in wage equivalents, the price of a slave in the past varied from one annual wage total for an agricultural or manual worker to three annual wage totals, while in the Indian debt bondage context of today, the equivalent is around twelve percent of the local annual wage rate of a farm laborer (one of the lowest paid workers in India).

The same trend applies elsewhere in the world today: in Ivory Coast, a slave costs just under four percent of the annual wages of a poor farm worker. This is more than a ninety-five percent fall in price. The price index score of four in the year 1856 would be equal to about $40,000 today, while in 2001, in Ivory Coast, agricultural workers are sold for about $40 each. Or in Thailand, where rapid economic change has led to new poverty and desperation, a girl aged twelve to fifteen can be purchased for $800 to $2000. The costs of running a brothel and feeding the girls are relatively low, especially considering how little they are fed. A girl will be told she must repay four times her purchase cost to gain her freedom – plus rent, food, and medicine costs. Even if she has sex with ten or fifteen men a day, her debt will keep expanding through false accounting. Her annual turnover, the amount men pay for her, is more than $75,000. The profit for the slaveholder is often as high as 800 percent a year and can be generated for three to five years.

This new, cheap form of slavery has developed over the last fifty years and several trends account for its emergence. First, the fall in slave prices is tied to the population explosion after World War II – a product of many positive events, including the control of infectious disease, better health care for children, and a prosperity that provided sustenance for the coming billions. As shown in figure 7, the world population exploded from two billion people to over six billion in about fifty years, and most of this growth was in the developing world. Many of the countries of the Global South now have population profiles that are heavily weighted to the young. For example, nearly fifty percent of Africa's population is between the ages of five and twenty-four, indicating that the momentum for further population growth is considerable. Worldwide there are now 426 cities with populations of more than one million people, and most of these are in the developing world – Mumbai alone has twenty million inhabitants. And in spite of large-scale migration to urban areas in the Global South, population pressure in rural areas also remains severe.

As the market was flooded with potential slaves, this led to a crash in prices, as shown in figure 8. Population growth therefore helps to explain the drop in slave prices. But it still does not necessarily explain the growth in slave numbers. Simply having a lot of people doesn't make them into slaves: another factor is poverty. Significantly increased populations do not in and of themselves create the possibility of enslavement, rather they increase pressure on resources, exacerbating impoverishment if an increase in productivity does not match this population growth. This impoverishment in turn renders people more suceptibile to enslavement.

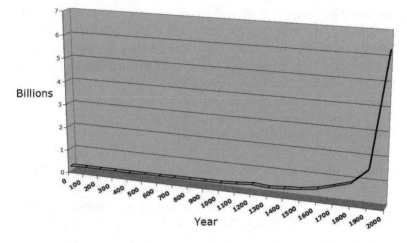

Figure 7 World population growth since 1 ad

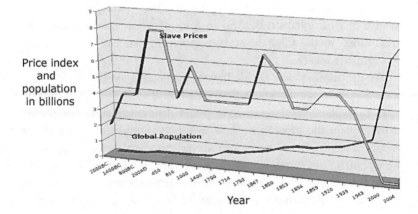

Figure 8 Population growth and slave prices, 2000 bc to 2004 ad

Poverty and debt

One factor pushing these growing millions toward slavery was the very economic growth that was supposed to make their lives better. The economic transformations of first modernization and then globalization have driven many people in the developing world both into the shanty-towns surrounding the major urban centers and into serious social and economic vulnerability. These dislocated and impoverished people are a bumper crop of potential slaves.

Like the world population, the global economy boomed after 1945. As colonies in the developing world became independent countries, many of their economies opened up to the spread of Western businesses. The economy became global and grew exponentially, bringing many benefits. But some parts of the world had no part in that growth. Throughout the world, whole populations were left behind, stuck in the subsistence poverty of the past or an even worse destitution.

In fact, the rapid change in the global economy has increased the poverty and vulnerability of large parts of the population in the developing world. Throughout Africa, Asia, and much of South America, the last fifty years have been scarred by civil war or wars for independence from colonial powers, and the wholesale looting of resources by leaders and elites who were often supported by the powerful nations of Europe and North America. Countries with little to sell on the world market have been put deeply into debt to pay for the weapons that leaders – often dictators – use to hold on to power. Meanwhile, traditional family farming was largely abandoned to concentrate on raising cash crops that could be sold to pay off those foreign debts.

So as the world economy grew and became more global, it had a profound impact on people in the Global South and the small-scale farming that supported many of them. The loss of common land shared by all the people in a village, and government policies that pushed down farm income in favor of cheap food for city workers, have helped to bankrupt millions of peasants and drive them from their land. All across the developing world the slums and shanty-towns that surround big cities hold millions of these displaced people. They come to the cities in search of jobs, but find they are competing for jobs with thousands of other displaced people. With little income and no job security, they are powerless and very vulnerable.

The foot of the ladder has two levels of poverty. On the very bottom rung are more than one billion people who live on $1 per day or less. All of these people are living in the developing world. For the most part, they are also living outside towns and cities, playing out the same hand-to-mouth existence that was the rule for most of human history. What does it mean to be this poor? The economist Jeffrey Sachs describes it like this:

> Extreme poverty means that the households cannot meet basic needs for survival. They are chronically hungry, unable to access health care, lack the amenities of safe drinking water and sanitation, cannot afford education for some or all of their children, and perhaps lack rudimentary shelter – a roof to keep the rain out of the hut, a chimney to remove the smoke from the cook stove – and basic articles of clothing, such as shoes.

This is life without options. Every action must be aimed at day-to-day survival, and even that goal may be unattainable. Desperation is the norm, and families are ready to do anything to survive.

One step up are families living on $1 to $2 per day; this is sometimes called "moderate poverty." Many of these families are living in the vast shanty-towns that surround the major cities of the developing world. For example, Mexico City has a population of twenty million, and about half of this number live in shacks and lean-tos of cardboard and scrap wood without basic services. Many of these families are economic refugees from rural areas that have been converted from family farms into plantations growing cash crops for export.

Their lives as subsistence farmers, based around the village and church, were shattered when they were dispossessed of the land their families had often worked for generations. Searching for jobs, they migrated to the city only to find themselves competing with millions of others. In the shanty-town they have lost the neighbors, the church, and the customs of the rural village. Criminal gangs control much of the slum. The government has little time or attention to give these poor and unregistered citizens, relegating them to second-class status. This pattern is repeated across the developing world and the result, whether in Rio, New Delhi, Manila, or Bangkok, is extreme vulnerability.

Some national and global policies also threaten these vulnerable and displaced people. The US government, for example, pays $19 billion a year to subsidize American farmers. It gives $4 billion a year to cotton farmers to help them grow a crop that is valued at only $3 billion. The cotton farmers in India, Benin, Mali, Burkina Faso, and Togo (all countries with high levels of slavery) cannot compete with this subsidy. Though they actually raise cotton at a lower cost than American farmers, the American farmers can beat them in the marketplace because they receive money from both the sale of the crop and from the US government. European countries pump money into the pockets of their own farmers as well, creating an unfair advantage on the world market.

When the global economy squeezes poor countries as it does with these farm subsidies, people have fewer and fewer options. Slavery can become one of the remaining options. Table 7 shows the

Table 7 Levels of poverty and levels of slavery for 193 countries

| | Amount of slavery in country | | | | |
	No slavery	Very little or rare slavery	Persistent, low level of slavery	Regular slavery in a few sectors	Slavery in many sectors
Extreme poverty	0	3%	49%	32%	16%
Moderate poverty	14%	17%	24%	17%	28%
Low income	21%	33%	39%	2%	5%
Middle income	30%	55%	10%	5%	0
Rich nations	20%	30%	30%	11%	9%

relationship between poverty and slavery in the world today. The table groups 193 countries according to poverty as measured by their Gross Domestic Product (GDP). It is easy to see that the poorest countries have the highest levels of slavery, and this would be a perfect pattern if were not for the effects of human trafficking. In the global market for people, the vulnerable are trafficked from poorer countries to richer countries. The result is that the richest countries have significant pockets of slavery.

The slow deterioration of an economy can also bring slavery in its wake. Most slavery occurs in the poorer parts of the world and many of these poor countries are poor because the citizens have lost control of their economies. Sometimes this happens when corrupt leaders take over a country. Such leaders are called "kleptocrats" and perhaps the champion kleptocrat was Charles Taylor, the former dictator of Liberia. Taylor stripped nearly all the wealth from the country, selling off its hospital equipment and even the desks and light fixtures from schools. Thousands of people were enslaved to dig diamonds at gunpoint. When he was finally driven from the country, he took $3 billion with him.

It is no coincidence that Liberia, with its high level of slavery, also has an international debt of about $3 billion. Many of the countries with high levels of slavery suffer from "debt overhang." The UN has classified thirty-eight countries of the world as being "high debt" countries, which means that these countries are carrying a crippling load of debt to international lenders. As Sachs explains, a high-debt country "must use its limited tax revenue to service the debt rather than finance new investments … Debt from the past crushes the prospects of growth in the future." Much of the national income has to go to pay back international banks.

The relationship between international debt and slavery is very clear. Countries with large debts cannot spend money on the things that are most likely to reduce the amount of slavery – schools, law enforcement, economic growth. Table 8 shows the link between international debt and slavery for 204 countries. The high-debt countries are concentrated in sub-Saharan Africa and include states with a high level of slavery such as Mauritania, Ghana, Niger,

Table 8 Levels of debt and levels of slavery for 204 countries

| | Amount of slavery in country | | | | |
	No slavery	Very little or rare slavery	Persistent, low level of slavery	Regular slavery in a few sectors	Slavery in many sectors
High-debt countries	3%	5%	42%	26%	24%
All other countries	25%	36%	26%	8%	5%

and the Congo. The persistent but low levels of slavery that exist in countries without a high debt reflects the fact that human trafficking carries slaves into the rich countries of North America and Europe.

While levels of poverty and national debt create a tough situation, this still doesn't automatically transform people into slaves. Like population pressure, increased vulnerability does not, in itself, "cause" enslavement. To convert the abundant and vulnerable into slaves requires the third supporting factor: governmental corruption.

Corruption

The linchpin of slavery in many countries is government complicity or indifference. To turn someone into a slave means keeping them where the law can't protect them, and in some countries, including the US, this means locking up individuals and keeping them isolated. But when governments fail to maintain the rule of law, its citizens can become slaves. Table 9 shows the link between slavery and government corruption for 177 counties. An annual report by the organization Transparency International scores most of the countries in the world on their level of corruption, and they are grouped below into high, medium, and low levels of corruption. The pattern is strong and clear: more corruption means more slavery. When extreme economic, social, and political vulnerability in one part of the population is matched by the ability of another part of the

Table 9 Levels of corruption and levels of slavery for 177 countries

| | Amount of slavery in country | | | | |
	No slavery	Very little or rare slavery	Persistent, low level of slavery	Regular slavery in a few sectors	Slavery in many sectors
Low corruption	47%	53%	0	0	0
Medium corruption	33%	34%	22%	6%	5%
High corruption	4%	19%	44%	19%	14%

population to mobilize the means of violence and the "right" to exercise it with impunity, the result can be slavery.

This pattern is a special challenge when corruption becomes institutionalized. Because slavery is now illegal everywhere, the complicity of crooked police is a fundamental requirement for slavery to take root and persist. In Western Europe, Canada, and the US, slavery happens in spite of the efforts of law enforcement, but in many countries slavery grows because of the work of the police. A simple payment to the local police allows the use of violence without fear of arrest. Sometimes the police themselves will provide violence for an extra fee, acting as slave catchers, pursuing and punishing escaped slaves. The bribes pass up the chain of command and into the hands of politicians and government officials. Soon law enforcement is dedicated to protecting systematic law violation.

For example, one researcher has noted that Japanese police are "tolerant" of organized crime, and in a report on human trafficking to Japan written for the Organization of American States, the researchers note that "policemen return women, who came to seek help, to the traffickers ... it is almost impossible to escape." Slavery is both pervasive and officially ignored in Japan. Police corruption is also one of the biggest obstacles to reducing slavery in Thailand, where lucrative police commands are sold to the highest bidder and the regular payments from slaveholders join the flow of money from other criminals into the pockets of police and government officials. And in Moscow, a single monthly payment provides protection from government taxes, police investigation, fire, theft, vandalism, safety inspections, and parking tickets. The size of the payment depends on the size of the business and whether it is legal.

In India, within the debt bondage slavery system, corrupt police provide protection for the slaveholders and take bribes to thwart prosecutions. With sex trafficking, corrupt police officers help transport victims and protect their enslavers. It is not difficult to understand the pressure on Indian police to join the slaveholders. If a police officer's salary is $10 or $20 a month in a country suffering from high inflation, the opportunity to bring in an extra $100 per month is the difference between poverty and affluence. Taking the bribe is even easier when the police are urged to do so by their bosses. Landlords, moneylenders, and businessmen, the powerful citizens of the town or village, are likely to use slavery in their businesses. Since the enslaved are often migrants from somewhere else, members of a "lower" caste or class, or a discriminated ethnic or religious group, serving their interests will have few rewards and plenty of penalties.

If this sort of corruption is widespread, then national governments face an enormous task. Yet government complacency joins with police corruption to exacerbate the situation in India. Governments at all levels in India have consistently failed to arrest and punish traffickers and slaveholders in every type of slavery in the country. This is particularly pronounced with regard to the debt bondage system. More than twenty-five years ago India enacted an excellent law against bondage, setting a three year prison sentence and a fine for anyone who is convicted of forcing people into, or keeping them in, bondage. But of the hundreds of cases that have been prosecuted, no convicted slaveholder has ever served prison time. Today fines of just 100 rupees (less than $2) are common for those convicted, making a mockery of the law. Equally, while Pakistan enacted a strong law against debt bondage slavery in 1988, and a large number of cases have come to light, not a single offender has been convicted. The enslaved may be freed, usually through the actions of human rights organizations, but the slaveholders are never punished. Instead, the ex-slaves and their liberators are at great risk of retaliation and persecution.

Predicting slavery and its economic impact

We have, then, the ability to predict the existence of slavery in any one country. Increases in the average population and high debt, along with a high degree of trafficking and an increase in the political rights index (which is consistent with more abuses), will all increase the probability that slavery will be a regular feature in several economic sectors, other things being equal. On the other hand, increases in the GDP per capita and the Human Development Index, and decreases in corruption levels, all increase the probability that any one country will have no slavery, other things being equal.

If we can predict the presence of slavery in this way, can we also predict its economic impact? The answer is yes: the amount of slavery in a country is itself a predictor of the country's level of economic and human development. The alteration of the basic economic component of the slavery relationship has changed the way that slaves are treated and the way that they fit within local and global economies. But the unprecedented fall in the price of slaves has had numerous results outside slave/slaveholder relations as well. In particular, it has hindered the development of national economies: slavery today is a drag on economies, preventing their development.

In 2006, Robert Smith analyzed a number of possible factors that were already thought to increase or diminish human and economic development: corruption, level of democracy, the amount of internal conflict, the amount of the national debt, as well as the regional groupings of countries, sometimes linked to culture. The result was clear: in his statistical trials, in each region, it was slavery that best explained differences in human development between countries. Other factors also played a role, but slavery was more important than the extent of democracy, the level of national debt, the amount of civil conflict, or the level of corruption. Slavery not only ruins the lives of slaves, but is a major cause of a depressed economy, low levels of literacy, and shorter lifespans, for all citizens in poor countries.

Slavery distorts local economies in two crucial ways, ways that spread up the economic ladder and affect economic and social development. The first is that enslaved laborers can depress the wages of free laborers in the same economic sector in which they work. Most slaves today are used at the lower end of the production ladder, growing or processing raw materials. For the poorest workers who are not enslaved, enslaved workers represent severe competition. The second way that slavery distorts economies is by the removal of enslaved workers and their families from local economies as consumers. While it is true that slaveholders make profits from their enslaved workers and that they enjoy the benefit of those profits, they are not as likely to spend those profits in the ways that average workers do – on local food, housing, clothing, and so forth. Likewise, enslaved families are unlikely to buy school supplies, pay teachers, access medical care or other services that both are part of the local economy and benefit the community.

So while slaves may make a lot of money for slaveholders, they tend to be a drag on a country's economy. They contribute only a little to national production and their work is concentrated at the lowest end of the economic ladder, in the basic low-skill jobs that are dirty and dangerous. The value of their work is stolen and pocketed by criminals, who are less likely to spend it on necessities. Slaves are not able to acquire assets. Just as it is for free working poor, asset acquisition is a determining factor in their achievement of economic autonomy. Economically, then, except for the criminals, slaves are something of a waste. They contribute next to nothing to a country's economy, buy nothing in a country's markets. They are an untapped economic resource. As we combat poverty to end slavery, we also need to combat slavery to help end poverty.

Smith's analysis also showed that gender differences increased the power of slavery to explain human development. But what is the specific role of gender in shaping the landscape of modern slavery? What are the particularities of the slave experience for women? Chapter four examines the dynamics of bondage for the millions of women and girls enslaved around the world today.

Their own sufferings: modern slavery for women and girls

Slavery is terrible for men; but it is far more terrible for women. Superadded to the burden common to all, they have wrongs, and sufferings, and mortifications peculiarly their own.

Harriet Jacobs, 1861

There is no single face of female slavery. The origins of women's enslavement are varied, and include poverty and sexual abuse at home or within marriages, kidnappings, and fake offers of jobs abroad. Their experiences of slavery are equally varied, ranging from blackmail, social isolation, thefts of their passports, and forced drug addiction, to beatings, torture, mock executions, private and public rapes, starvation, forced marriages, abortions, depression, enslavers' threats to kill their families, and multiple re-sales between different slaveholders. And their lives after slavery all look different, including attempts to support their children, decisions to enter prostitution, time in prison, rejection by their families, and HIV infection. Kaew, who was trafficked from Thailand into slavery in Japan, explains the sheer diversity of experiences: "If you talk to different women, you will get very different stories."

Yet, in spite of this vast range of experiences, a sense of the shared impact of slavery runs throughout women's narrated stories. Nu, who was also trafficked into Japan from Thailand, argues for a general impact of forced prostitution on women: "No one in the world can get over sleeping with one man after another who does not love you." Seven months pregnant at the time of her testimony,

Nu offers a statement of despair for all girls born into her world: "I am waiting to give birth to my baby. I hope it is not a girl. She must not suffer like me." Similarly, Dina, who was trafficked within Cambodia, sees in her own life "the situation of thousands of Khmer women and other women around the world." Female slaves have a "situation" in common. But what *is* this "situation"? What do the many faces of female slavery look like today?

Forced prostitution in the West

The most well-publicized form of international trafficking is that of women into forced prostitution. At least half of international trafficking cases are for sexual exploitation and, while women account for fifty-six percent of forced economic exploitation, they account for ninety-eight percent of forced sexual exploitation. Many of these women accept job offers and sign phony contracts, beginning the journey into slavery. Told they owe money for their trip, they must work off the debt with clients. Slaveholders use violence, starvation, and social isolation to retain control. And there is often a double bind: not only of the brothel owner's restrictions, but the restrictions of a foreign country where they cannot speak the language, have no knowledge of their legal rights, and often fear the police.

Most are taken from poorer countries to richer countries, with many thousands arriving in Canada, the UK, the US, and Western Europe. For example, women arrive in Canada from South Korea, Thailand, Cambodia, Malaysia, and Vietnam, and most are trafficked for commercial sexual exploitation. The Royal Canadian Mounted Police conservatively estimates that between 800 and 1200 people, most of them women, are victims of human trafficking in Canada each year. In the UK, the Home Office recently announced that of the hundreds of people who had been trafficked into the country in just an eighteen-month period, seventy-five percent of them were women and girls.

In the US, around eighty percent of the foreign-born individuals trafficked into the country each year are female, and seventy percent of these women end up in forced prostitution. Feeder countries include Albania, the Philippines, Thailand, Nigeria, and Mexico (many from the central region of Tlaxcala, a haven for slave traders). Major trafficking organizations are Asian criminal syndicates, Russian crime groups and syndicates, and loosely associated Latin American groups. Many women are lured from their home countries by false promises of legitimate employment in the US, and they are primarily trafficked in three ways: the illegal use of "legitimate" travel documents, imposter passports, and entry without inspection. The women are forced to work to pay off the debts imposed by their "smugglers" – debts ranging from $40,000 to $60,000 per person. They might perform 4000 acts of sexual intercourse each year to meet their quota, at $10 to $25 per act. In other situations, girls as young as twelve years old are forced to have sex seven days a week, with ten to fifteen people a day, and meet a quota of $500–$1000 a night.

Estimates of the number of people who are trafficked within and into Europe annually range from 100,000 to 500,000, and human trafficking is Europe's fastest-growing criminal activity. By some estimates, ninety percent of non-national women active in the sex industries of south-eastern Europe have been trafficked. But most women are brought from the poorer eastern countries to the richer West: over two-thirds of trafficked women from former Soviet countries end up in Western Europe. The UN ranks Belgium, Germany, Greece, Italy, and the Netherlands "very high" as destination countries, and Albania, Bulgaria, Lithuania, and Romania "very high" as origin countries.

This process of trafficking from eastern to western countries began when socialism was dismantled in the USSR in 1991. "Transition countries" (nations that moved from socialism to capitalism) saw an explosion in the export of men, women, and children as slaves. The transition period in most of the ex-socialist countries has been marked by economic recession, hyperinflation, high unemployment, and armed conflict – prompting large numbers of refugees and economic migrants to seek entry to Western Europe. Traffickers make false promises of employment and corrupt border guards reportedly accept bribes to facilitate trafficking. As many as 100,000 women are now trafficked from and throughout the fifteen former Soviet countries annually and sold into international prostitution.

In Russia, tens of thousands of women are trafficked each year to over fifty countries for commercial sexual exploitation. One key overland corridor into the European Union is the "Eastern Route" through Poland. The women arrive in Central and Western Europe and also the Middle East. In Israel, women arrive from Russia, and also Ukraine, Moldova, Turkey, Uzbekistan, Lithuania, Belarus, Brazil, Colombia, and South Africa. Officially, the estimate of trafficked women each year in Israel is 3000, and in 2006, the UN ranked Israel "very high" as a destination country for trafficking.

The fall of socialism in 1991 also led to a rise in organized crime in Albania, which is currently one of the top ten countries of origin for sex trafficking. Albania suffered badly from the interruption of trade with countries of the Eastern block after 1989. In 1991, its GDP was only half that of 1990 and half of all children were malnourished. Over the next ten years, an estimated 100,000 Albanian women and girls were trafficked. Today, more than sixty-five percent of Albanian sex-trafficking victims are minors at the time they are trafficked, and perhaps fifty percent of victims leave home under the false impression that they will be married or engaged to an Albanian or foreigner and live abroad. Another ten percent are kidnapped or forced into prostitution. The women and girls are commonly tortured if they do not comply.

From Armenia, women are trafficked to the UAE, where an estimated 10,000 women from Eastern Europe, sub-Saharan Africa, South and East Asia, Iraq, Iran, and Morocco are victims of sex trafficking. Armenian women are also taken to Greece and Turkey, where victims arrive from Ukraine and Moldova as well. Moldova is another main country of origin for the trafficking of women and children into European sexual exploitation. Again, the country's economic conditions fuel this trafficking. In 2000, the country's GDP was forty percent of its level in 1990. Moldova has the lowest average salary of countries in the former Soviet Union, and women's salaries are seventy to eighty percent of those of men. Unemployment remains extremely high, especially among women –

who comprise around seventy percent of the unemployed – and more than half the population lives below the poverty line. Consequently, women are forced to look outside of the country for work and pimps take advantage of these migrants, though some victims are kidnapped. Thousands of women have been trafficked out of the country in recent years. Most Moldovan trafficking victims are taken to the Balkans and other destinations include Asia, Western Europe, and the Middle East.

The push for women to leave Ukraine is equally powerful. There, they account for up to ninety percent of the unemployed and are usually the first fired. Traffickers abduct an estimated 35,000 women from Ukraine each year, and in 1998 the Ukrainian Ministry of Interior estimated that 400,000 Ukrainian women had been trafficked in the past decade, although Ukrainian researchers and NGOs believe the number is higher. Ukrainian consulates have brought 11,000 trafficking victims back to Ukraine, and the International Organisation for Migration (IOM) says it has helped more than 2100 Ukrainian victims since 2000, but adds that this is a small portion of the total number. Almost fifty countries serve as destination points throughout Europe and eastward. Germany is one of the most popular destinations in Europe for women trafficked from Ukraine, though victims also come from Africa (mainly Nigeria) and Asia (mainly Thailand).

Forced prostitution in Africa and Asia

While we have estimates for the number of trafficking victims in Europe and the US, the number of people who are trafficked around and out of African countries remains unknown. We can, however, identify some patterns. The UN notes that victims trafficked from African countries frequently arrive in Ivory Coast, Nigeria, and South Africa, and that those trafficked out of Africa arrive in the UK, Italy, France, Belgium, the Netherlands, and Saudi Arabia. Trafficked women and children arrive in South Africa from Angola, Botswana, the Democratic Republic of Congo (DRC), Lesotho, Mozambique,

Malawi, South Africa, Swaziland, Tanzania, Zimbabwe, and Zambia. Several major criminal groups in South Africa now traffic women: Bulgarian and Thai syndicates, the Russian and the Chinese Mafia, and African criminal organizations, mainly from West Africa. Women are trafficked through false promises of employment, marriage, or education, and some are simply abducted.

The UN ranks Nigeria particularly high as an origin country for human trafficking, and Benin, Ghana, and Morocco slightly less high. Around 45,000 Nigerian women have become victims of trafficking over the past fifteen years (two-thirds have gone to Europe and a third to the Gulf States). We know, too, that thousands of Ethiopian girls are trafficked into Lebanon each year for sexual exploitation, and that Zimbabwean women are forced into prostitution in the UK and the US. Zimbabwe's trafficking problem has worsened since 2005, when the Zimbabwean government began Operation Murambatsvina ("Clean-Up"), a campaign to forcibly clear slum areas. This has displaced hundreds of thousands of people, and left an estimated 223,000 children, especially girls, vulnerable to trafficking.

Yet more often than for sexual exploitation, individuals are trafficked from Africa for forced labor: thirty-five percent of reported trafficking cases in Africa are for forced labor, according to the UN. In Asia, however, only twenty percent of reported human trafficking cases are for forced labor, and the greater majority is for sexual exploitation. The IOM estimates that around 225,000 women and children are trafficked every year in Asia. In Southern Asia, Sri Lankan women are trafficked to Saudi Arabia, Kuwait, the UAE, Bahrain, and Qatar for sexual exploitation. And in Nepal, up to 12,000 women and children (many aged between nine and sixteen) are trafficked every year across the border into India. An estimated 200,000 trafficked Nepalese women and girls currently reside in Indian brothels and Nepal has an unknown number of internal sex trafficking victims as well.

India's National Crime Records Bureau reports that there are 9368 trafficked women and children in the country, though, acknowledges that a sizeable number of crimes against women go unreported due to the attached social stigma. The Central Social

Welfare Board of India has published much higher figures, for example estimating that up to one million women and children were being used in forced prostitution in six metropolitan cities in India, and that within this group, thirty percent had been enslaved when they were younger than eighteen.

In Southeastern Asia, Cambodia is ranked high as an origin country for trafficking by the UN. Prostitution escalated in Cambodia when the UN Transitional Authority Forces arrived in 1991. The number of prostitutes in the cities rose from 6000 in 1991 to 20,000 in 1992, and the Cambodian Women's Development Association claims that half of these women were trafficking victims. Women continue to be internally trafficked for sexual exploitation, usually from rural areas to the country's capital, Phnom Penh, and other secondary cities, and are also sent to Thailand and Malaysia for forced prostitution.

The UN ranks Thailand even higher as an origin country, and it is the only country in Asia to be ranked "very high" as an origin, transit, and destination country. Thai women and girls are lured from rural areas with the promise of work in restaurants or factories. The slave-recruiter offers the girls' parents an "advance" on their wages, but then they are enslaved and sold to a brothel. The brothel owners tell the girls that they must pay back their purchase price plus interest through prostitution, though they typically don't let them go until they can no longer be sold to men because of physical or mental breakdown. The brothels do have to feed the girls and keep them presentable, but if they become ill or injured, they are disposed of.

Thousands of women are also trafficked annually out of Thailand for sexual exploitation. The major destinations include Japan, Malaysia, Bahrain, Australia, Singapore, and the US. In Singapore, women and girls are also trafficked from Indonesia, Malaysia, the Philippines, Vietnam, and China. And in Japan, women are also trafficked from the Philippines, Russia, and Eastern Europe, and on a smaller scale from Colombia, Brazil, Mexico, Burma, and Indonesia.

The sale of sex in Japan is a vast industry. Japan is by far the richest country in Asia and the region's largest destination for trafficking – the only country in Eastern Asia that the UN ranks "very high" as a destination country for human trafficking. The US State Department agrees. In its 2004 "Trafficking in Persons Report," Japan appeared in the same group as poor, war-torn countries like Serbia, Tajikistan, and Ivory Coast, and was in danger of being classified in the worst tier, where sanctions can apply. The Japanese population is one of the most law-abiding in the world, with a robbery rate of 1.3 per 100,000 people compared to a rate in the US nearly 180 times greater. Yet slavery flourishes in Japan. Currently, the cost for sex in a "fashion massage" shop is $50 to $90. Moving down the ladder, sex with foreign women is sold on the street for $8 to $10. By 2001, the Japanese sex industry was thought to generate $20 billion per year and was known to be rapidly growing.

A conservative estimate of the total number of foreign women enslaved as prostitutes in Japan is 25,000. In addition, while the marriage rate of Japanese women to foreign men has remained fairly constant, marriages of foreign women to Japanese men have sky-rocketed to more than 30,000 a year. An investigation by the Organization of American States explained that while many of these marriages are legitimate, some are known to be "phony marriages arranged by traffickers and used to move foreign women into the Japanese sex trade or the underground labor force."

Thousands of the foreign women in Japan are on over-stayed visas and tourist visas, and as Nu explains, it was easy for her enslavers to manage the problem of over-stayed visas:

> Sometimes the police would come in to check if there were visa-overstayers. The owner was mostly warned in advance by informants. Overstayers would be concealed, or heaped into a bus and hidden in a hotel close by in the mountains 'til the police left. At other times the bar would be closed for a day or two. There was also a time when only those with valid visas were produced before the police, and the police bribed.

According to government estimates, there were about 220,000 illegal residents who had over-stayed their visas in the country in

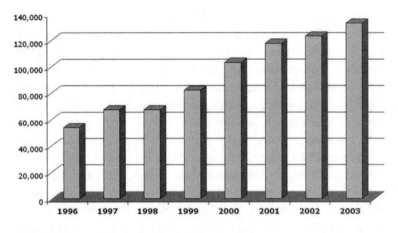

Table 10 Entry into Japan on "entertainer" visas

2004, and hundreds of thousands more will arrive each year on tourist visas. Both categories will contain a significant number of women held against their will. But another part of Japan's slavery problem is its euphemistically titled "Entertainment Industry," which includes brothels, strip clubs, bathhouses and street prostitution. The government has a special "entertainer visa," supposedly given to singers and dancers that will be giving performances in theaters and nightclubs. If this were true, then Japan would have more professional entertainers than the rest of the world combined.

In reality, the visa is used to import large numbers of foreign women to meet the demands of Japanese men for sex and "entertainment." Between 1996 and 2003, the number of visas issued each year more than doubled (see table 10).

In 2003, approximately 80,000 "entertainers" came from the Philippines and, over the years, around 40,000 women have come from Latin America on entertainer visas. Under intense pressure from human rights groups and other countries, Japan finally agreed to better police the entertainer visa system from March 2005, but no figures have been released showing a fall in the number of "entertainers" brought to Japan.

The Japanese government does not ignore all exploitation of women, however. In the late 1990s a scandal rocked the country: over the last decade, some Japanese schoolgirls had been practicing enjo kosai, or "compensated dating." Using their mobile phones, girls between the ages of fifteen and seventeen would arrange dates with older Japanese men. The dates could simply be for coffee or could include sexual contact, and the girls were paid for their time. Surveys of high school girls suggested that as many as one in five had engaged in compensated dating. The girls, almost universally, explained that they wanted the compensation to buy designer clothing and pay cell phone bills. The controversy exploded when a girl was beaten, sodomized, and infected with a sexually transmitted disease on a compensated date. Much of the Japanese public's shock came from the fact that middle-class schoolgirls were involved. Legislation was immediately enacted and protections were put in place, while, at the same time, thousands of foreign women, many the same age as the Japanese schoolgirls, remained trapped in forced prostitution.

Prostitution

The scandal over "compensated dating" in Japan points to the often-confused relationship between prostitution and forced prostitution. While the Japanese schoolgirls were children – and under international law no child can consent to being sexually abused – cases of adult prostitution are more controversial within the anti-slavery community. This controversy centers on whether all prostitution should be considered a form of slavery.

On one side of this issue are people and groups, including some feminist organizations and faith-based groups, who believe that all women who sell sex are slaves. For example, The Coalition Against Trafficking in Women (CATW), based in the US, argues that all prostitution is forced in some way, either by violence or social or economic pressures, and that no person would freely choose to become a prostitute. By this logic, prostitution, like slavery, needs to be abolished, and CATW demands that prostitution and sex trafficking be fused together in legislative responses. Arguing against the legalization of prostitution, they point to places where prostitution is legal, such as Germany, the Netherlands, and some Australian states, and argue that legalization creates a situation in which criminals can more easily operate. Other anti-prostitution advocates include the Protection Project, Equality Now, and Planned Parenthood Federation of America.

On the other side of the controversy are organizations focused on human rights, public health, labor, and migration, including the Global Alliance against Trafficking in Women, and the Network of Sex Workers Project. They recognize a difference between forced and voluntary prostitution, and contend that some, but not all, prostitution is slavery. As one group of NGOs put it in 1999, "An adult woman is able to consent to engage in an illicit activity (such as prostitution). If no one is forcing her to engage in such an activity, then trafficking does not exist." Some advocates on this side have maintained that if prostitution is the best of the available choices, then women should be protected and allowed to engage in "sex work." And some promote the legalization of prostitution, arguing that if the government is in control of prostitution, it can regulate and oversee it. If prostitution is legalized, it comes out of the shadows and into the open. The legalization of prostitution, to those on this side of the debate, lessens many of the dangerous aspects of sex work and makes cases of forced prostitution more readily identifiable.

Ann Jordan, director of Global Rights' Initiative Against Trafficking in Persons, also points out that while "current federal law enables prosecutions of all enslavers and provides protection for all victims," the broad scope of the law "equates prostitution with trafficking, and is redirecting resources to end prostitution rather than to end trafficking." She suggests that the investigative and prosecutorial arms of the federal government are being diverted from their primary goals of eradicating all types of slavery, in order to pursue a war on prostitution.

There is some agreement between the two sides of this debate. Everyone agrees that non-consensual or forced prostitution is slavery and must be stopped. Everyone agrees that no minors should engage in prostitution. And both sides of this debate are carefully watching the results of a new law in Sweden, where prostitution was previously legal. Under the new law the sale of sex is legal; it is the purchase that is made illegal. The criminalization of only the purchase attempts to redress the imbalance of power between men and women. In passing the law, the Swedish parliament viewed the economic and social relationship between a woman selling sex and a man buying it as unequal, and held that men's ability to buy women's bodies could be seen as a form of male dominance to be resisted and controlled.

This approach is unique, and runs counter to recent laws in Germany and Holland that attempt to reduce the demand for women trafficked into prostitution by legalizing and regulating brothels. For example, prostitution was legalized in Germany in 2002, in part to stop slavery. As a legitimate trade, prostitution would presumably be safer and healthier. But the UN still rates Germany "very high" as a destination for sex-trafficked women – primarily from central and eastern Europe – and in 2006 the European Parliament expressed concern that there would be an increase in sex trafficking prior to the commencement of the 2006 World Cup (though there was eventually no evidence that this occurred).

Sweden is trying to extinguish the demand for prostitution and trafficking at the point of consumption. Germany and Holland are instead trying to reduce enslaved prostitutes in the supply chain by arresting traffickers. At this point, no one knows for certain if either approach is working. Criticism has been leveled at the Swedish law for pushing prostitution underground and toward trafficking victims, but there is as yet no evidence to support this. The Swedish government states that the law is reducing the number of women exploited in prostitution, but again little evidence is available. Similarly, the legalization of brothels in the state of Queensland, Australia has been interpreted as both decreasing and increasing slavery.

Domestic labor

In China, sexual exploitation combines with forced domestic labor, forming the practice of forced marriage. The practice is mainly internal, though reports exist of women kidnapped from

Vietnam and North Korea, and is attributed, in part, to the country's one-child policy. Introduced in 1979, the policy has resulted in sex-selective abortions when a fetus is female, leading to gender imbalance in the population. Men who live in communities where there is a shortage of women have resorted to purchasing brides kidnapped from other areas. One report by the UN Special Rapporteur on Violence against Women observes that the kidnapping and sale of women has increased since the mid-1980s and that forced marriage accounts for thirty to ninety percent of marriages in some Chinese villages. Once married, the women have no freedom of movement, are raped, and forced into domestic labor.

In fact, though it is less well publicized than sex trafficking, the enslavement of women and girls into domestic labor is widespread around the world. Zimbabwean women are brought from rural to urban areas for forced domestic labor, and thousands of Sri Lankan women – as well as women from Malaysia, Indonesia, the Philippines, Somalia, and Ethiopia – are trafficked into Lebanon for domestic servitude in private households. They often enter Lebanon legally but then find themselves trapped. For example, at the age of twenty-three, Beatrice Fernando responded to an advertisement for work as a housemaid in Lebanon. She left her home country of Sri Lanka, intending to send money to her parents and her three-year-old son. But in Beirut she became a domestic slave:

> At the job agent's office in Beirut, my passport is taken away … Lebanese men and women pace in front of us, examining our bodies as if we were vacuum cleaners. I am sold to a wealthy woman, who takes me home to her mansion up on the fourth floor of a condo building. My chores seem unending. I wash the windows, walls, and bathrooms. I shampoo carpets, polish floors, and clean furniture. After 20 hours I am still not done. There's no food on my plate for dinner, so I scavenge through the trash. I try to call the job agency, but the woman who now owns me has locked the telephone. I try to flee the apartment, but she has locked the door.

Guards were instructed to shoot her if she tried to leave, and she eventually escaped by jumping from the apartment's fourth floor balcony.

The majority of domestic slaves, however, are children. Globally, domestic work is rarely scrutinized or legislated, and statistics are hard to obtain. But the ILO estimates that at least ten million children, some as young as eight, are trapped in domestic labor around the world. This form of slavery is estimated to be worth $7 billion per year, and some ninety percent of domestic slaves are girls aged between twelve and seventeen. There are 700,000 child domestics in Indonesia, 560,000 in Brazil, 300,000 in the Philippines, 300,000 in Bangladesh, 265,000 in Pakistan, 200,000 in Kenya, and 100,000 in Sri Lanka. The children work fifteen or more hours a day, seven days a week, for little or no pay under abusive conditions, generally have little or no freedom of movement, are denied schooling, and are often sexually exploited. Consequently, domestic work is often a precursor to commercial sex work.

There are also millions of enslaved domestics in India, where children are frequently sent away from their villages to work in order to clear a family debt. These loans have immensely high rates of interest, and in many cases no remuneration is given at all. The debt is often passed onto a younger sibling or onto the domestic's own children. Many domestics in India – some as young as seven or eight – are on duty around the clock, sleep on the kitchen floor, eat leftovers, and have no holidays or rest breaks.

This form of slavery is a problem in the world's richer nations as well: it is the second highest incidence of forced labor in the US, fueled by the demand for cheap, exploitable household help, the lack of legal protections in the domestic service sector, and the absence of monitoring of work conditions. The thousands of domestic slaves in the US include women from Brazil, Ivory Coast, Ethiopia, Nepal, Ghana, and India, and their vulnerability is increased by an immigration policy that allows domestic workers to be brought to the US by their employers. Visas normally require that domestic service workers remain with their original employer or face deportation. This requirement tends to discourage workers from reporting abuses.

For example, Roseline Odine and Christina Elangwe (see figure 9) spent two and a half years and five years respectively as domestic slaves in Washington DC, held by fellow Cameroonians. Promised American educations and babysitting jobs, they were tricked into leaving their families in Cameroon at the ages of fourteen and seventeen. But upon arrival in the US, they weren't sent to school. As Christina explains, "the agreement was that as soon as I came here I would start school. I came in the month of February … That whole year passed and they didn't send me to school … The following year came and I asked them. They said I should wait." Instead, they worked long hours for no money: "It was seven days a week," remembers Christina. "I did everything from five in the morning until maybe midnight or 1am. I had to get up, get the kids ready, give them showers, make their breakfast, keep on doing household jobs like cleaning, cooking, everybody's laundry, ironing, and when the kids came back from school I gave them lunch … They never paid me anything." The women were beaten and verbally abused, and Roseline was sexually harassed. To Christina, the fact of her former enslavement is clear: "I consider myself a slave because I

Figure 9 Roseline Odine and Christina Elangwe

worked for so many hours without getting paid, and without going to school. And I couldn't leave."

The women's captors were eventually convicted. Roseline's were sentenced to nine years in prison, and told to pay her $100,000 in restitution. Christina's captors received five years probation and were ordered to pay her $180,000 in back wages. And both before and after these convictions, numerous other cases have emerged in the US. In May 2006, the US Justice Department announced the conviction of a Wisconsin couple for enslavement. According to the charges, they had held a woman in a condition of servitude for nineteen years, requiring her to work long hours, seven days a week. They had threatened her with deportation and imprisonment if she disobeyed them, and forced her to hide in the basement when people entered the house. The government convicted the couple on forced labor charges, and harboring an undocumented alien. In November 2006, the two individuals were sentenced to each serve four years in prison.

Beyond the US, the UK and Europe have an unspecified number of domestic slaves. For about six years, from the age of twelve, Mende Nazer was beaten, sexually abused, fed food scraps, and kept prisoner as a domestic slave for a family in the Sudanese capital of Khartoum. "I had to do very hard work," she remembers now. "I had to do everything: clean the house and big yard, wash clothes by hand and look after her children ... I was beaten for every single thing." At the age of nineteen she was taken to London and passed onto the family of a Sudanese diplomat, where she was instructed to "obey the new master and do the same sort of work I did [in Sudan]."

Seba experienced domestic slavery in France, after leaving her home country of Mali at the age of eight. A couple took her to Paris, promising her parents that they would educate and care for her, in return for work as a nanny. But instead she was enslaved, beaten, tortured, and forced to do domestic chores:

> I was not sent to school, I had to work every day in their house. I
> did all the work; I cleaned the house, cooked the meals, cared for
> the children, and washed and fed the baby. Every day I started work
> before 7am and finished about 11pm. I never had a day off. My food

was their leftovers … If I took food she would beat me … She beat me with the broom, with kitchen tools, or whipped me with electric cable.

Seba was freed when a neighbor heard the sounds of abuse and beating, and managed to talk to her. Seeing her scars, the neighbor called the police and the French Committee against Modern Slavery (CCEM).

Women enslavers and liberators

Seba remembers pronounced mistreatment at the hands of her "mistress," rather than a "master." As she recalls, it was the woman in the house who was wholly invested in the institution of slavery. In fact, the broader role of women in enslavement and trafficking challenges the simple image of men enslaving women. Women play a significant role as the enslavers of adult and child domestics. As well, the percentage of female traffickers is rising. Some have been trafficked themselves and then – with a detailed background in the mechanism of trafficking – reappear on the trafficking scene voluntarily as recruiters or pimps. Others are blackmailed, or are forced to engage in recruitment to reduce their own debt to traffickers. Often, female traffickers are the most convincing at deceiving women and girls into accepting fake job offers and beginning the journey into slavery.

For example, in China, women are increasingly becoming involved in trafficking operations, especially in identifying and abducting victims. Many of the female recruiters are former victims themselves. In India, many traffickers are older women. Some are former prostitutes and others are still in forced prostitution, trying to escape by providing a substitute. Data from one report shows that around fifty percent of people involved in the trafficking process in India are female. Another report explains that women comprise two-thirds of traffickers in Cambodia, while in Japan, women operate the bars that function as brothels – as Nu explains. Recruited by a hairdresser friend in Thailand, she was held by a "mama" (female brothel manager): "The mama warned me not to try to run away as she would be very tough, and that all girls who tried escaping were brought back and severely beaten or sold." And in numerous other testimonies by Thai women trafficked into Japan, the initial recruiters and then the enslavers are female. Nuch's experience was typical:

> At Narita airport immigration, the agent told me to go to a specific line and she went in another one ... Then we took a taxi to a hotel in Tokyo. She told me I would work at a Thai restaurant that belonged to a Thai woman named Ice ... They told me there was no way out and I would just have to accept my fate ... Ice beat me, mostly by kicking me everywhere ... The mama's daughter slapped me when I was told to serve a very rude, drunk and dirty client whom I had been forced to have sex with several times before and couldn't stand it.

From the female agent, Nuch was handed to Ice, then to a Taiwanese "mama," and was even abused by the brothel manager's daughter.

In the Western Balkans overall, more than a quarter of all traffickers are women – mostly engaged in cross-border trafficking – and in Albania and Bosnia Herzegovina, over half of all recruiters are women. In Moldova, more than half of all people involved in the trafficking process are now women. Alana was trafficked from Moldova to Russia, and remembers that it was a woman who locked her up and forced her into prostitution, while Milena, another Moldovan woman trafficked to Russia, recalls the role of a girl named Dolina, who persuaded her to take a job as a nanny: "She told me we could make $400 or $500 each month, and the work was not very difficult ... In Moscow, we went to an apartment building ... I asked Dolina: 'Will I baby-sit here?' She told me: 'Yes, in this place.'" Soon afterward, Dolina vanished, five Russian men arrived, and Milena was forced into prostitution.

At the other extreme, however, are occasions where women are central to the process of liberation. Irina, who was trafficked from Russia to Germany, describes one woman's attempt to help her: "A beautiful Russian girl by the name of Tatiana helped me try to run away by stealing my fake passport and all of my real documents from the pimps ... But I later learned that she was killed for helping me." And in 2000, when some of the 220 residents of Sonebarsa (a quarrying village in Uttar Pradesh, India), revolted against their slaveholders, women were central to this process of self-liberation, as the women themselves explain. Choti observes that women "played a very big role in getting revolution," and Shyamkali explains that "because we are also bread earners ... we also have equal role to play in fighting for our freedom."

But beyond the direct role of women in the processes of enslavement and liberation, gender is tightly connected to modern slavery in a multitude of culturally specific ways. Distinguishing between the terms "sex" (biological distinctions) and "gender" (socially constructed roles for men and women), we can examine slavery through a gender lens and find different vulnerabilities, impacts, and consequences for women.

Supply and demand

Gender shapes both slavery's supply and its demand. The gender dynamic of supply is multifold:

- When ideologies of women's secondary status are present alongside extreme poverty, it creates a lethal combination that permits their bodies to be regarded as commodities. For example, the social practice of dowry payment in Nepal means that a girl's parents must offer gifts to the spousal family that could be worth several years' income. Offering a good dowry would be crippling and daughters are perceived as a liability, so when an opportunity presents itself, poor families in particular may be willing to trade unwanted women and girls as a viable survival strategy. Traffickers are particularly successful in persuading parents to hand over their daughters when they offer false prospects of "dowry-less" marriage.
- Women's lower-valued social role excludes them from the workforce. In many countries, particularly in rural communities,

women are confined to the unpaid care economy in the household. Lacking a paid economic role, they are dependent on male relatives, and the death or unemployment of those relatives, or the withdrawal of economic support, renders them vulnerable. For example, Anita, who was trafficked from Nepal to India at the age of twenty-seven, describes her vulnerability: "Last year my husband took another wife. Soon after, he began to beat me, torment me, and disregard my children. I decided it would be best if I and my children moved out of our home. I made money by buying vegetables from farmers and selling them in the village market." Anita was trafficked when she boarded a bus on a trip to sell her vegetables and accepted food from another passenger. The food was drugged and she woke up in India.

- When women do engage in paid employment, their choices are narrowed by the social requirement that they only undertake a limited range of "women's" occupations – which tend to be lower paid. Even in richer nations, women hold a second-class status. In Japan, few women are employed above the lowest levels; the first woman to ever be named to run a major corporation took up her post in 2006. Women are paid significantly less than men and the country has no legal recourse for systematic discrimination against women, whether by the government, businesses, or other institutions.

- Women's unequal access to education further limits any opportunities to increase their earnings. In a male privileged culture, women and girls receive less education than men and boys, and are more often withdrawn from school to assist in household management and family care. Poor, unskilled women workers are the first to suffer retrenchment and unemployment in a declining economy. Made vulnerable by a lack of job opportunities and education, women caught in this feminized poverty and gender inequity can be more easily tricked by traffickers who hold out false promises of employment.

- Some traditional community attitudes and practices tolerate violence against women. Around the world, abuse, incest, domestic violence, and marital disintegration can make women and girls more desperate to escape their situations, and therefore willing to risk trusting a trafficker. In Japan, domestic violence only became illegal in 2002 and police routinely ignore complaints of assaults on women by their husbands. Equally, the low status of women in Zimbabwean society perpetuates gender violence. And in India, traffickers manipulate girls by playing on the realities of gender-based violence, sexual exploitation, or the fear of a repugnant marriage. One recent report showed that, of the reviewed women enslaved in Mumbai, almost half reported some type of family disruption as directly leading to their trafficking; predominantly violence involving husbands or other family members. The report concluded that the "interaction of poverty and gender-based mistreatment of women and girls in families heightens the risk of sex trafficking."

All these factors – the dowry practice, dependence on male relatives, lack of job and educational opportunities, and violence – come together in India, especially in the state of Uttar Pradesh, where many thousands of trafficked women are brought from villages in the state of Bihar. Here, gender roles that disadvantage women economically increase their vulnerability to enslavement. Cultural norms associate sons with economic advantage and daughters with the burden of dowry. Often women are paid in grain rather than money, and when they are paid they receive less than men and have fewer economic opportunities to increase earnings. Other work opportunities away from the village are also less available. So when men leave the family, cannot work, or when they fail to send money home, women have great difficulty supporting their families.

Meanwhile, gender bias in India often means that girls are not allowed to attend school. Girls have constant and recurring domestic work obligations, such as caring for animals and collecting firewood and cow manure for fuel, leaving little time to attend school. Limited opportunities at home, coupled with the substantial burden of household labor, can lead to girls running away or being lured by young men who promise marriage. When girls are trafficked, it is often through taking advantage of a girl's aspiration for a life outside domestic drudgery. And finally, Indian women who experience abuse or abandonment by their husbands often face community ostracism. Families may be reluctant to offer support, based on fears of additional negative consequences for their status, and other support options are limited.

If these supply factors are shaped by gender around the world, so too are demand factors. As one researcher explains, trafficking and slavery are "fuelled by a supply of women denied equal rights and opportunities for education and economic advancement" and driven by a "demand for women's and children's bodies." The demand for "bodies" reflects not only the growth of the billion-dollar sex and entertainment industry, but also for the increasing tendency for foreign workers to fulfill domestic and care-giving roles in richer nations. For example, in newly industrializing countries, such as Singapore and Hong Kong, educated middle-class women have entered the workforce, raising the demand for foreign domestic help. Yet sex-selective migration policies and restrictive emigration laws limit women's legal migration, as the UN explains: "Women's vulnerability to trafficking is greater because of the lack of avenues for legal migration." As well, women often have less access to information on legal migration opportunities and a greater lack of awareness of the risks of migration, compared to men.

These factors mean that women are more likely to seek alternative routes of migration and try to enter a country through illegal channels, which puts them at risk from traffickers. The ILO confirms that trafficking declines when there are more opportunities for regular migration. Noting that "liberalizing entry conditions enables potential victims to avoid trafficking risks," it cites a reduction in trafficking among women from EU accession countries immediately after the lifting of visa requirements.

Gendered slave experiences

Once trafficked and enslaved, women continue to encounter a range of gendered abuses – from forced plastic surgeries to forced abortions and sexual violence. Christine (see figure 10), who was trafficked

Figure 10 Christine Stark

within the US, recalls a process whereby her enslavers used sexual violence to divide and conquer women: "They rape us in front of our mothers and grandmothers; they rape our grandmothers and mothers in front of us … They want us to feel like it is our fault that our mother, sister, daughter, grandmother is being destroyed in front of our eyes. They want us to dislike and distrust other women and girls." And for many women, this process of violent induction into slavery includes a change in their social status as women. Anita remembers that she was marked as a "prostitute": "They cut off my hair … Now that I had short hair, I knew that I could not leave the brothel without everyone identifying me as a prostitute. In my culture, short hair is the sign of a wild woman."

Rita, who was also trafficked from Nepal to India, adds that some women feel so marked that they refuse to escape:

There are so many other sisters in the place where I was sold. I told them we shouldn't stay there. "Let's go! We will go to Nepal instead. We shouldn't do this kind of work, let's go," I begged. The newcomers agreed to come, but the girls who had been there for 15–16 years didn't want to come. When the police arrived I begged them to leave the place. "Let's go, let's not stay here," I said. But they said they wouldn't go. "What will we get if we go to Nepal? We'll get nothing but misery. We've been sold like this, we've become prostitutes. We will not be accepted by society. We won't go," they said. "Even if we go, we will go only with money." And even the policemen who came to raid said they will take only those who wish to go.

In fact, Rita describes a series of experiences that are deeply rooted in her identity as a woman. The traffickers tricked her by explaining that they needed her to help smuggle diamonds – because "girls were not checked as thoroughly as men" by border guards. One of the first incidents in India is the replacement of her trousers for a long skirt. And she describes the horror for women of public questioning about experiences in slavery:

> We were harassed by lawyers and police after we come back to Nepal. The way they question – it is like scratching a wound. They question us as if we went knowingly. "They have done this willingly," that's what they think. We have come back from that sort of place with all the pain and suffering, and even then we have to file a complaint with the police. The men there question us and ask: "How many did you sleep with?" After I came back from there, when I went to the Jawalakhel police station and a man was writing down the complaint, there were many boys and other men present. Those policemen should have thought about how awkward it would be for this girl, being questioned like that in the presence of everyone, but they don't ... They shame us in public. It's more painful because of this.

Nepali girls and women are more likely to be arrested than rescued by the police, and female law enforcement officials, who are rare in India and Nepal, are untrained in crimes against women, leaving women like Rita without the option of approaching another woman about the experience of slavery.

Rita's memory of public shame after slavery is echoed by Alina, who was trafficked from Armenia to the UAE. She describes public discrimination after her liberation through a police raid: "The most shameful thing happened at Yerevan airport. Everybody was treating me as if I were a prostitute, saying bad words. My life has changed since that time. Now you see me here in the street. I have become a real prostitute." Unable to reenter mainstream society, women are at risk of being retrafficked or else may choose – like Alina – to enter sex work.

The post-slavery experiences of Rita and Alina point to yet another gender-specific aspect of slavery: once they have escaped from slavery, women returnees face a greater stigmatization than men. This rejection comes not only from strangers, but from the women's families, as Anita explains:

> When I first went home to my family, it was very uncomfortable. The people in the village laughed at me. In my culture, a woman is scorned if she is missing for just one night. I had been missing for two months. It was very hard for my family, especially since we are members of the Brahmin caste. So, today I live in Kathmandu. I work as a domestic servant in the city. I am still without my children since they went to live with their father when I was taken away. I am told that my husband's new wife is very cruel to my children, but my husband does not want my children to be with me because of where I have been.

Indian and Nepalese families tend to deny atrocities against women to protect family honor, and those women who insist upon speaking out – or even those who don't – are often shunned by their families.

This means that most Nepalese victims never leave India, even after liberation. One researcher noted in 2006 that "many will stay in India, aware from others of the lack of support and welcome they will receive on returning." He added that the women who do return "face an uncertain future of rejection, institutionalisation, and extreme poverty or, in despair, a return to prostitution … [T]he causes of rejection are again based on the 'dirty goods' notion in Nepali society, whereby any girl who has lost her virginity outside of marriage for whatever cause is seen as worthless." Many women who return to Nepal remain in shelters in Kathmandu.

Women are particularly vulnerable to trafficking because of systemic gender-based inequalities around the world. As Gillian Blackell explains, "the unequal status of women in families and society, the feminization of poverty and harmful stereotypes of women as property, commodities, servants and sexual objects are among some of the root causes of trafficking in women." The UN Special Rapporteur on Violence against Women adds that the "lack of rights afforded to women serves as the primary causative factor of [trafficking in women] ... Economic, political and social structures ... have failed women." But if gender inequality shapes the landscape of modern slavery so profoundly, do other identity differences have the same negative power? Chapter five examines slavery through the lens of race, ethnicity, and religion.

5

Of one blood: racial, ethnic, and religious aspects of modern slavery

[The] slave-holder's rule contradicts this fundamental truth of God's word, that "God has made of one blood all the nations of men," and if of one blood, they are of equal blood.

Jonathan Blanchard, 1845

At moments in the long history of slavery, the otherness of slaves has made it easier for slaveholders to maintain total control with violence and cruelty. In the nineteenth-century American South, the racist element of slavery was so strong that a very small genetic difference, being one-eighth black and seven-eighths white, meant lifelong enslavement. Similarly, in a fusion of slavery and religion, people from across the Muslim world would bring a slave on their religious pilgrimage to Mecca and sell the slave upon arrival to help finance the trip. This continued into the early twentieth century. Today, slavery is less dependent on racial, ethnic, or religious difference. Though race, caste, tribe, and religion might initially look like determinants of slavery, most often these differences simply make people vulnerable to slave traders: behind most assertions of difference is the reality of economic disparity. Most slaveholders feel no need to explain or defend their use of slavery, and use other criteria to choose slaves. The question is not "are they the right race or religion?" but "are they vulnerable or gullible enough?"

Certainly, some cultures are more divided along racial lines than others – for example, Japanese culture strongly distinguishes the Japanese as different from everyone else, and so enslaved prostitutes in Japan are more likely to be Thai than Japanese. But even here, the key difference is economic. Japanese women are not as vulnerable and desperate, and Thai women are available for shipment to Japan because Thais are enslaving Thais. Yet while racial, ethnic, or religious differences do not wholly define modern slavery in most countries, they do remain at its heart in a few, and are used as justification in several others. In Niger, Mauritania, Ghana, India, Thailand, Nigeria, and China, perceived differences of race, ethnicity, and religion still form the dividing lines between slaves and the free.

Hereditary slavery

Most slaves today enter slavery during their lifetimes, through a variety of methods that include kidnappings and false promise of employment. But around the world there are millions of other slaves who have been born into their situation. In the African countries of Niger, Mauritania, Mali, and Chad slavery is still racialized and hereditary. In Niger, where slavery is a centuries-old practice, there are perhaps 43,000 individuals who were born into slavery. These slaves are from four of the country's eight ethnic groups, are controlled through violence and indoctrination, and are separated from their parents at a young age. Slavery was outlawed in Niger in 1960, when the country claimed independence from France, but this has remained a theoretical ban.

Women and girls perform domestic duties, men tend herds of cattle and goats, and children are often passed from one owner to another. Tamada (see figure 11), who was born into slavery in Niger, describes her life as a hereditary slave:

> I was born into slavery, like my mother and grandmother. I was separated from my mother when I was very little ... I worked everyday since I can first remember. I was always moving; pounding

millet, washing, cooking. I worked from dawn 'til late after dark, collecting firewood and fetching water ... As I got older I began to look after my mistress's children and then I had to do all the household chores ... My master used to beat me often.

Tamada escaped in 2003, at the age of eighteen. That same year, slave-holding in Niger was made punishable by up to thirty years in prison. But the new law has made little difference. In September 2004, the Tuareg chief Arissal Ag Amdague made a written promise that he would release 7000 slaves owned by his people. Claiming that his religious beliefs as a Muslim were incompatible with slave-holding, he said he wanted to release the slaves he had inherited. The date was set for this first ever mass release of slaves in Niger: 5 March 2005, at a ceremony in the village of Inates. But no mass emancipation took place. Instead, on 5 March Amdague stood before the crowd and denied that he owned any slaves.

Figure 11 Tamada

The racism of "old" slavery has also persisted in Mauritania. The population of Mauritania is divided into three main groups: the ruling Arab Berbers (or Moors), slaves and the descendents of slaves, called the Haratine, and several tribal groups of Black Africans, normally called Afro-Mauritanians. The Arab Berbers have owned chattel slaves for generations. Born into bondage, slaves and their children are the property of male family members. Slave families usually live within their master's household, are not paid for their work, and have no freedom of movement. They begin work at an early age and typically herd livestock, tend crops, and perform domestic duties.

Selek'ha Mint Ahmed Lebeid and Oumoulkhér Mint Mahmoud were born into slavery in Mauritania. Selek'ha explains that she was inherited as property and passed between "masters":

> I was taken from my mother when I was two years old by my first master … he inherited us from his father … When I was very small I looked after the goats, and from the age of about seven I looked after the master's children, and did the household chores – cooking, collecting water and washing clothes … When I was 10 years old I was given to a Marabout, who in turn gave me to his daughter as a marriage gift, to be her slave. I was never paid, but I had to do everything, and if I did not do things right I was beaten and insulted.

Selek'ha escaped in 2000 at the age of twenty after she realized she was a slave: "I felt my situation was wrong. I saw how others lived," she explains. Then, with the help of the human rights organization SOS Slaves, Selek'ha returned to seek the release of her mother, Oumoulkhér.

But for Oumoulkhér, leaving slavery was more difficult. She initially refused to leave her master:

> I have been a slave all my life. I was a good slave … When Selek'ha came for me, I refused to go, because I am an old lady and useless, but then the master's wives started to insult her and Selek'ha was crying so it made me angry and I decided to leave. Selek'ha has promised to look after me.

Oumoulkhér's initial reluctance to accept her freedom because she is "an old lady" symbolizes this ancient and deeply rooted form of slavery. The practice of buying, selling, and breeding people as slaves has existed in Mauritania since the thirteenth century, when Arab invaders entered the country to convert the Africans to Islam, abducted women and children, and bred a new slave "caste." Today, the institution of slavery remains deeply ingrained in the social structure and culture of the country – as Salma explains. Born into slavery in Mauritania, she observes that many slaves can't even imagine escaping:

> I was born a slave … My mother and father were slaves for one family, and their parents were slaves … I always thought about liberty. The other slaves were afraid of being free. They were afraid that they wouldn't know where to go or what to do or who to talk to … I know many people who are still slaves there, from my family and other families. I never knew people in my family who escaped before me. In my family, I was the first one. My mother and father died slaves.

Some slaves are "afraid of being free" and all are raised to believe that serving their Arabo-Berber masters is a duty. Most remain in bondage their whole lives.

Slavery was first abolished in Mauritania in 1905, by colonial French rulers, and again when Mauritania joined the UN in October 1961. It was abolished for the third time in 1981 by the Military Committee of National Salvation. But the situation didn't fundamentally change. As one social scientist observes, the legal framework was not "sufficient to abolish the status [of slaves], which is inscribed in a complex web of economic, ideological and symbolic relations." There was no provision for enforcement, masters still didn't have to pay their slaves or provide any sort of social security, and the ban did not address how masters were to be compensated or how slaves were to gain property.

This arrangement allowed the legal fiction of slavery's abolition to continue. Then, in 2003, Mauritania passed a law that made slaveholding punishable by fines and imprisonment. But no slaveholders were prosecuted. "It doesn't matter what the laws say there, because there they don't apply the laws," observes Salma. "Maybe it's written that there is no slavery, but it's not true." Until 2007 the government officially maintained that slavery did not exist and actively suppressed any attempt to expose it, prohibiting the media from using the word "slave." Anti-slavery activists were jailed for their activities. The official denial of the situation made it difficult to calculate how many slaves there were in the country, but estimates generally ranged from 20,000 to upwards of 400,000.

In 2007 the situation in Mauritania dramatically altered. The elderly President for Life was deposed in a bloodless coup, and replaced with a caretaker government that delivered fair and free elections. Anti-slavery activists and ex-slaves were encouraged to run for office and several achieved government positions. By late 2007 the newly elected government had begun working with international anti-slavery groups to plan the eradication of slavery. New laws criminalized slavery and slaveholders were charged and put on trial for the first time.

Ritual slavery

Just as racialized slavery has been a long-standing tradition in Mauritania, so a religion-based slavery has existed for centuries in a different West African nation: Ghana. The system of *trokosi* (a Ewe word meaning "wife of the gods" or "slave of the gods") is prevalent among two patrilineal groups, the Ewes of southern and northern Tongu and Anlo, and the Dangmes of Greater Accra. Local organizations estimate there are between 5000 and 20,000 Ghanaian women currently held as *trokosis*, predominantly in the rural Volta region. Children under the age of ten comprise a tenth of the total number. The *trokosi* practice also exists to a lesser extent in the West African countries of Togo and Benin, and in southwestern Nigeria.

This ritual slavery revolves around atonement. Fetish priests who run shrines insist that only by handing over a virgin daughter – typically aged between eight and fifteen – can families atone for alleged offenses committed by their relatives or ancestors. These offenses can range from murder to petty theft. Once the girls are handed over, priests turn them into slaves and impregnate them repeatedly. They are beaten when they try to escape, and are denied education, food, and basic health services. Most remain in slavery for between three and ten years, some for their whole lives. If they die, the family must offer another virgin daughter, and if they are ever released, former *trokosis* are considered unmarriageable. Like slavery in Niger, the *trokosi* system is hereditary: any children born to a *trokosi* become slaves, and *trokosis* are passed on to the next priest upon one priest's death.

Between 1996 and 2006, the group International Needs-Ghana freed 3500 slaves from over 130 shrines in the Volta and Greater Accra regions of Ghana. But close to ninety percent of the 2000 *trokosis* liberated between 1997 and 1999 returned to the shrines. Facing stigma from their families and communities, and boycotted if they tried to sustain themselves economically, their independence meant starvation. As well, some remained fearful of repercussions for disobeying the gods.

The *trokosi* practice was banned in Ghana in 1998, but enforcement of the ban has been ineffective. Some Ghanaians argue that the children of *trokosis* are destined to redeem mankind. Others argue that the *trokosi* system maintains order in place of law enforcement. Still others insist that *trokosis* are priestesses, not slaves. Most vocal is the Afrikania Renaissance Mission, which says the practice upholds the religion of their forebears and cites article 21 of the Ghanaian Constitution (guaranteeing freedom of religion). Togo and Benin have done little to stop the practice, and practitioners in Ghana now bring girls from these countries.

A similar system exists in South Asia. Nepal has the *deuki* ("girl offered to god") system, which involves around 17,000 girls. Rich families without daughters buy young girls from impoverished, rural families and offer them to temples as their own. They are dedicated as servants to temple deities, prohibited from marrying, and often engage in prostitution to support themselves. Even more widespread is the *devadasi* ("servant to the gods") system in India, part of a Hindu tradition. Pre-pubescent girls are dedicated to the Goddess Yellamma by family members and village elders, given to temple priests, and sexually enslaved. They begin sexual servitude between the ages of eight and twelve, and remain the property of the priests well into adulthood. Family members undertake dedication out of devotion to the goddess, fear of her disapproval, and hope that the offering will ease a family crisis. The practice is prevalent in two Indian states in particular: Andhra Pradesh, where there are around 17,000 *devadasis*, and Karnataka, where there are around 23,000. It was banned in Karnataka in 1984 and in Andhra Pradesh in 1988, after which the total number of *devadasis* declined. But by the early 1990s there remained around 50,000 *devadasis* in Karnataka alone.

Declared as "wives" of the gods, *devadasis* are prohibited from making normal marriages. Instead they are available for sex with the deity's priests or devotees and become the temporary concubine of one man after another. This temporary "husband" is under no formal obligation to support his d*evadasi* or any children she may bear. Some provide a temporary room, but most *devadasis* live with their parents. Traditionally, *devadasis* lived within the temple grounds but this is no longer a widespread arrangement. They are not paid for sex and instead must support themselves through low-skilled labor in agriculture or construction. Once the period of sexual activity is over, by middle age, a stigma remains. The *devadasi* status can never be cast off and the inability to make an ordinary marriage usually means extreme poverty for the rest of the *devadasi's* life. Children of *devadasis* also suffer discrimination because they have no recognized fathers. Sometimes the *devadasi* role is passed on to the new generation, but more often the children simply become vulnerable to commercial sexual exploitation.

Nearly all of India's *devadasis* belong to "scheduled castes" – people in the lowest social categories who exist outside the formal caste system. Previously know as "untouchables," today these people are known as "*dalit*." No *devadasi* comes from an upper caste. And in fact, beyond this supply of *devadasis*, India's caste system creates a ready-made hierarchy for numerous other forms of enslavement.

Ethnic and religious hierarchies

Though officially outlawed, India still has an internal Hindu "caste" system – a hierarchy of social differences ascribed at birth. According to India's 2001 census, the "scheduled castes" population is close to 170 million persons, constituting around sixteen percent of the country's total population. Caste discrimination shapes all political, economic, and social relations. The people of the lowest caste, the *dalit*, are segregated, and denied access to land, education, and employment. By tradition, *dalit* people are assigned community tasks (cleaning, plowing, removal of animal and human waste) and must perform this labor without payment or face eviction, ostracization, and violence.

The *dalit* people form a large proportion of India's slaves. While members of the same caste may be both slave and free, the caste system is such a strong social and cultural feature of Indian society that one NGO terms it an important factor "behind the trafficking of women and children." At least eighty percent of all bonded laborers in India come from the most discriminated castes, as do most child laborers trafficked from Bihar, seventy percent of child domestic workers in Chennai, and around sixty percent of Indian victims of forced prostitution. In particular, the states of Uttar Pradesh and Bihar remain "traditional" on the ideology of caste. Here, caste discrimination is compounded by cultural practices, especially among the Bedia tribes in Uttar Pradesh who force their first-born daughter into prostitution. One result of this practice is that Bedia families reportedly kidnap infant girls to raise as their first-born daughters and then prostitute them at about age nine.

In fact, around the world, individuals who belong to marginalized groups – whether indigenous peoples, tribal groups, refugees, or migrants – are targeted for trafficking and enslavement. For example, in the oil-rich states of Saudi Arabia and Kuwait, Muslim Arabs enslave Sri Lankan Hindus, Filipino Christians, and Nigerian Muslims. And the tendency to target marginalized groups has an ethnic component, too. In individuals' home countries, ethnic discrimination can be a root cause of migration, and therefore put people at risk from traffickers. In Romania, Bulgaria, and Albania, being a member of a minority group such as the Roma is a risk factor, while in Nepal, most Nepalese slaves are from the hill ethnic groups (such as the Tamangs, Magars, and Sherpas) and lower castes. In Thailand, most Thai slaves are from the northern hill-tribes who do not possess Thai citizenship. Facing social exclusion and economic exploitation, ethnic hill-tribe women and girls are more vulnerable to enslavement.

Ethnic discrimination also determines the treatment that individuals receive after migration. For example, ethnic Russians in Latvia and Estonia have difficulties finding formal employment. This problem of discrimination in the formal labor market for minorities puts them at higher risk for trafficking. One UN report explains that, more generally, women trafficked into Western Europe from Central and Eastern Europe face racial discrimination as "foreigners," and other research suggests that forced domestic labor can be linked to the desire to demonstrate one's position in a racial or ethnic hierarchy.

Just as ethnic differences are a factor in supply, so are they a factor in demand. Women trafficked in the Balkan region are priced depending on their skin color and racial characteristics, and in 2003, the IOM reported that clients visiting brothels in Thailand "typically placed different groups on different rungs of a racial or ethnic hierarchy." These hierarchies are shaped by "the social devaluation of darker skin, which is widely associated with dirt, lack of sophistication, and peasantry." Darker women from Burma and North Thailand were at the bottom, and therefore cheaper. And alongside its internal caste system, slavery in India is marked by a hierarchy of skin color too. The IOM reports that dark-skinned women and girls were at the bottom of this hierarchy, and white Europeans were at the top. Devalued in this way, darker-skinned individuals are more likely to be forced into prostitution.

So while not defining slavery to the same extent as hereditary bondage in Mauritania, race and ethnicity do play a role in slavery's supply and demand. So too does religion. In numerous countries around the world, religion forms the dividing line between slave and free without wholly defining the system of bondage. Beyond its role in creating social exclusions and economic vulnerabilities, as in India's Hindu caste system, or in shaping ritual slavery, as in Ghana and India, religion is a weapon for traffickers and slaveholders adept at applying its doctrines.

Religious justifications

Traffickers and enslavers use religion to facilitate their activities, without turning bondage into a wholly religious ritual. For example, in Pakistan, religion is not the defining factor in enslavement, yet many enslaved brick makers are Christians and many slaveholders are Muslim. In Nepal, cases of slavery are higher in Muslim areas – not because Islamic doctrine demands a slave system, but because divorced women are often seen as outcasts and can easily be coerced away from their villages and forced into prostitution.

In Thailand, slaveholders draw on another world religion: Buddhism. First, one application of Buddhism justifies male promiscuity and the use of prostitutes. Seeming to sanction prostitution, the "*vihaya,*" or rules for monks, lists ten kinds of wives and the first three are "those to be enjoyed or used occasionally." Second, Theravada Buddhism, which is the most widely practiced form of Buddhism in Southeast Asia, positions women as inferior to men. Women cannot reach the state of nirvana, and being born a woman suggests a particularly sinful previous life. Slaveholders encourage women and girls to believe that they must have committed terrible sins in a past life to deserve their enslavement and abuse. Third, adapting yet another Thai cultural belief based on the teachings of Buddhism – acceptance and resignation in the face of life's pain and suffering – slaveholders urge the women to accept their karmic debt, to come to terms with it and to reconcile themselves to their fate. They can prey on young women even more effectively when these applications of religious tradition combine with the view of some parents in rural, poor areas that their daughters are commodities, and also the belief held by Thai children, especially girls, that they owe their parents a profound cosmic and physical debt.

Thai slaveholders' use of religion to encourage acceptance of enslavement is echoed by Nigerian traffickers in Europe. Here, traffickers apply West African voodoo to discourage women from attempting escape. After accepting an offer of work in Western Europe, and before leaving Nigeria, women and girls undergo an initiation ritual. This can include the marking of their faces and hands, the laying of hands on a "*juju*" (statue), and the drinking of blood. Their hair and nail clippings are often placed in a magical pouch that gives the slaveholder control over their soul. They are made to swear to the gods that they will work hard for their employers, and will never mention their real names, run away, or contact the police. Once in Europe they are drugged and sold – most often to brothels. If the women are not cooperative after arrival, they may be exposed to a mixture of physical violence and new, enforcing rituals. Captors, usually the brothel "madams," threaten the women with death or punishment by the gods for disobedience, and warn that any attempt to escape will awaken a curse on their families.

An orphan who was tricked into leaving her village in northern Nigeria in 1998, Joy Ubi-Ubi, remembers that she drank blood during a voodoo ritual. Afterwards, once she was in Europe, her captors said this ritual meant the *juju* would kill her if she tried to escape. As Joy explains, she was thereby "forced" to become a prostitute:

> We went very far – before, I had only been to the next village or to the market. When we got there I met some men in white clothing. There was a woman there too, a priestess ... They asked me to pull off my shoes, and they brought blood for me to drink. They asked me to drink it for my own good, and said that it wasn't going to kill me. I drank it, and they marked my body and my hand. Then they gave me a sheep's eye and said I had to eat it ... They said that anybody who was going to Europe had to do this ... When I was finished, they asked me to put my hand on the *juju* ... Then they took me away in a car, and straight into a ship ... In the Red Light District I said: "what kind of job is this?" They said, "prostitution" ... One man said that if I went to the police, or if the police arrested

me, they would deport me to Nigeria, and then he would come to
Nigeria by himself to kill me … They said that because of everything I drank before coming, and because I had put my hand on the
juju, if I went to anybody or tried to run away, the *juju* would kill
me. So I was forced to do the work..

Joy was enslaved for three years in the deprived Bijlmer district of
Amsterdam, home to many West African immigrants. She made the
decision to escape after she became pregnant and was told to abort
the baby.

A very different fusion of religion and slavery occurs in China.
While Thai slaveholders adapt Buddhist teaching to condition
women into accepting enslavement, and Nigerian traffickers apply
voodoo to prevent them from attempting escape, the Chinese
government uses religious belief as justification for prison labor.
Over the past twenty years, much of China's national prison system
has been converted into a system called the *Laogai* ("reform-
through-labor"). Created by the Chinese Communist Party in
the 1950s under Mao Zedong, the *Laogai* system is intended to
"reeducate criminals" and uses prisoners as a source of cheap labor.
Within the *Laogai*, there are three primary institutions: convict labor
reform camps ("*Laogai*"), re-education-through-labor camps
("*Laojiao*"), and forced job placement ("*Jiuye*"). The Laogai
Research Foundation has identified 1045 camps across China and
estimates that these camps currently hold more than one million
people, while the ILO puts the figure at 260,000.

The camps are really factories, which produce major consumer
goods for the lucrative export market and pay no salaries. Each camp
has both a prison name and a public name; for example, the
Shanghai Municipal Prison is also called the Shanghai Printing and
Stationery Factory. And while it might seem reasonable that
convicted criminals, serving their sentences, should work to pay
their keep, that is far from the situation – especially in the *Laojiao*
camps. Prisoners in *Laogai* camps may have been formally arrested,
tried, and sentenced, but *Laojiao* does not require legal proceedings.
The *Laojiao* component of the *Laogai* system was revived in the early

1980s and gives the government the right to arrest and detain dissenters without a formal charge or trial for up to three years. Ramin Pejan explains the government's use of *Laojiao*:

> [China] uses *Laojiao* to detain individuals it feels are a threat to national security or it considers unproductive ... Because those in *Laojiao* have not committed crimes under PRC law, they are referred to as "personnel" rather than prisoners and they are not entitled to judicial procedure. Instead, individuals are sent to the *Laojiao* following administrative sentences dispensed by local public security forces. This vague detainment policy allows the PRC to avoid allegations that the individual's arrest was politically motivated and to assert that they were arrested for reasons such as "not engaging in honest pursuits" or "being able-bodied but refusing to work."

People can be arrested and imprisoned without trial for "crimes" such as professing a forbidden religion or expressing opinions in disagreement with the government. These prisoners have never been to trial, have no right to legal representation, and once imprisoned have no rights or protections. They work for up to sixteen hours a day and experience solitary confinement, torture, gang rape, sleep deprivation, malnutrition, drugging, and brainwashing.

The "threat to national security," as Pejan puts it, often translates into any opposition group, such as Tibetans who object to the Chinese occupation of their country or practitioners of Falun Gong – a spiritual movement based on Buddhist principles and Daoism that was banned in China in 1999. Falun Gong practitioners are often targeted for arrest, along with ethnic minorities, Catholics, Protestants, and Tibetans. Sam Lu (see figure 12), who was imprisoned in 2000, observes: "I was arrested in China only because I handed in a letter at the State Appeal Bureau in Beijing to express my opinion about Falun Gong." He was jailed for two months and "forced to work on export products such as toys and shopping bags without pay." Describing his living and working conditions, he notes: "The cell was only about 300 square feet in size, with 20 prisoners and one toilet inside. They slept and worked in the cell. Sometimes we were forced to work until 2 AM to keep up with the schedule."

Figure 12 Sam Lu

In September 2007, the US State Department observed that Falun Gong practitioners "continued to face arrest, detention, and imprisonment, and there were credible reports of deaths due to torture and abuse." It added that practitioners who refuse to recant their beliefs are "subjected to harsh treatment in prisons, reeducation through labor camps, and extra-judicial 'legal education' centers." Estimates of Falun Gong practitioners who have spent time in the *Laogoi* system usually range from 10,000 to 100,000 persons, though in 2005 the US House of Representatives heard testimony that at least half of the 250,000 officially recorded *Laojoi* inmates are Falun Gong adherents.

China is not the only country where the government, rather than an underground trafficker, uses religion as justification for enslavement. In Sudan, thousands of people have been taken into slavery during the decades of the country's civil war. Slave-taking was revived in 1985 by the National Islamic Government of Sudan, as a weapon against insurgents in the South. Women and children were given Arabic names, and some of the women were circumcised: while the purpose of enslavement was not Islamization or Arabization, the government abused Islamic conceptions to continue slave-raiding activities in the name of the Holy War of Jihad.

Here is a situation where religion combines with armed conflict to produce enslavement. But what further role does war play in modern slavery? Does war always involve slave-taking? What kind of labor do the slaves perform? Do post-conflict nations experience a higher proportion of slavery? And if conflict zones are hot-spots for slavery, what about a different kind of regional pressure – environmental destruction? Does slavery itself cause damage to the environment? Chapter six examines the relationship between slavery and the regional factors of war and environmental destruction.

6

Subjugated soldiers, terrorized terrain: armed conflict and environmental destruction as factors in modern slavery

Subjugation of the slave as a soldier ... would be right and proper ...
The use of slaves as soldiers is ... justifiable.

Henry S. Foote, 1864

The late twentieth century and early twenty-first century have seen slavery repeat some of its oldest historical patterns, coming full circle from ancient Babylonia to modern-day Bosnia. Human slavery was born in conflict, and wars still unleash slavery on threatened populations today. Almost every war generates slavery, and in 2003, for example, trafficking into slavery occurred in eighty-five percent of conflict zones around the world, including Colombia, Nepal, Sri Lanka, Burma, the DRC, and Sudan.

If armed conflict is a catalyst for slavery's growth, so too are environmental destruction and natural disaster. In some areas of the world, armed conflict combines with environmental destruction. Burma's military uses slaves for logging, which destroys the forests and raises funds for more armed conflict against rebel groups. Both the loss of forest land and the armed conflict in turn create a displaced population vulnerable to enslavement. And armed conflict also combines with natural disaster to increase slavery in a region, as with the tsunami disaster of 2004. This destroyed the northeast region of Sri Lanka, which had already been damaged by decades of civil war, and left women and children, in particular, even more vulnerable to traffickers amid a further loss of infrastructure and community cohesion. Around the world, slavery grows quickly amid the chaos of armed conflict, environmental destruction and natural disaster, because this chaos brings with it economic crisis and violence – two of slavery's key ingredients.

Displaced people

When people are impoverished, destabilized, and displaced through war, environmental destruction, or natural disaster, they are vulnerable to exploitation. Then violence, which runs wild when the rule of law breaks down in the face of these pressures, is used to convert the poor and vulnerable into slaves. Most vulnerable are displaced individuals. Civil war, ethnic conflict, and invasions create millions of refugees and internally displaced people, whose precarious situations make them susceptible to being trafficked. Poor, exposed to health risks, and in unfamiliar circumstances, they have little capacity to secure work and are more likely to accept a trafficker's false promise of employment.

For example, in Afghanistan, armed militias kidnap and traffic people, but the ongoing armed conflict also has a less direct effect on slavery: it increases migration, leaving female and child refugees exposed to traffickers. Equally, throughout the armed conflict in Nepal, incidences of internal trafficking have risen. A decade of Maoist and military activities had displaced 100,000 people by 2006, many of whom fled to the big cities or across the border into India, increasing their risk of being trafficked and enslaved. By 2002 in Sierra Leone, after eleven years of civil war, around ninety-five percent of displaced families had experienced sexual assault, including rape, torture, and forced prostitution. And across the whole African continent, decades of civil strife have displaced millions of people – approximately four million, according to the IOM – and left them vulnerable to enslavement.

The direct relationship between displacement and slavery was also clear when the country of Yugoslavia began to break up in the 1990s. Bordering Italy, Yugoslavia had been a stable and relatively prosperous country with modern health care and education systems. When it collapsed into civil war between ethnic groups, refugee women were captured and sold to slaveholders who forced them into prostitution. Slave markets appeared in the destroyed towns and cities. In February 2001, the International Criminal Tribunal for the former Yugoslavia announced sentences of twenty years for those found guilty of sexual enslavement during the conflict.

Displacement continues to impact the levels of trafficking and slavery once a conflict is over. During the last few decades, post-conflict nations – including the former Yugoslavia – have struggled against a rising tide of slavery. Europol notes that "civil wars in the former Yugoslavia ... were the pillars which underpinned anarchy, crime and economic poverty," and that now the conflict is over, "120,000 women and children are trafficked through the Balkans alone each year." The report adds that "before the war, there was no evidence of trafficking in this region." The large numbers of displaced families, refugees, and war widows, along with the lack of law and order and the damage to economies, political systems, basic infrastructure, and social networks, all create an environment in which trafficking and slavery can flourish.

Another reason for the disproportionately high rate of trafficking in post-conflict nations is the influx of peacekeeping forces and reconstruction personnel. There has been documented sexual exploitation of minors by peacekeepers around the world, sometimes involving girls as young as thirteen receiving food in exchange for sexual services. As the UN observes, trafficking for forced prostitution in Eastern and Central Europe has been increased by "the presence of thousands of international troops." This was the case in Kosovo in the late 1990s, and one study argues that sex trafficking was also rare in Sierra Leone, Somalia, and Cambodia until the arrival of international troops spurred a demand for trafficking victims.

In 2003, the US State Department anticipated that this pattern would be repeated in the aftermath of the Iraq war:

> Displaced persons, widows and other vulnerable women, separated children or orphans ... could gravitate toward peacekeepers and humanitarian workers as sources of potential income and safety only to be exploited for labor or sex ... As we have seen elsewhere, the demand for prostitution often increases with the presence of military troops, expatriates, and international personnel who have access to disposable income.

Sure enough, widespread trafficking, including abductions of displaced people, began in mid-2003. In 2005, the US Department of Defense investigated allegations that its contractors or subcontractors had enslaved displaced people, and concluded that low-skilled workers from Nepal, India, Pakistan, Bangladesh, Sri Lanka, and the Philippines had been trafficked in Iraq as well. In 2007, the US government added that South Asian men were being trafficked through Jordan into Iraq for forced labor.

But the phenomenon of trafficking in displaced people is even more pronounced in Colombia, where a forty-year conflict has displaced millions of people and created the second largest internally displaced population in the world, after Sudan. The war began in 1964, when government forces tried to destroy a leftist guerrilla movement, which later formalized itself as the Revolutionary Armed Forces of Colombia (*Fuerzas Armadas Revolucionarias de Colombia*, or FARC). Another large guerrilla group is the National Liberation Army (*Ejército de Liberación Nacional*, or ELN), and the government-backed umbrella organization for many paramilitary groups is the United Self-Defense Forces of Colombia (*Autodefensas Unidas de Colombia*, or AUC).

As one report notes, the war "has been a significant factor leading to the growth of modern day slavery." Colombia's economy has declined during the war, leaving sixty percent of the population living below the poverty line. Amid the chaos of the lawless environment, traffickers can easily take advantage of the poor and desperate. Most vulnerable are refugees and internally displaced people. More than three million Colombians have been displaced by the war. Most are internally displaced, living on the outskirts of their society, and of the 50,000 Colombians trafficked each year, at least fifteen percent are these internally displaced people. The remainder of the displaced people (upwards of 200,000) are refugees, including 75,000 in Ecuador and 75,000 in Venezuela. Barely any of these people have formal refugee status. Fearing they might not meet the status criteria, and so face a forcible return to Colombia, they do not apply. Again, displacement leaves them vulnerable to traffickers.

Forced displacement affects children in particular. Of the three million Colombian refugees and internally displaced people, around fifty percent are under eighteen years old. And as of 2006, up to 35,000 internally displaced children had been forced into prostitution across Colombia. As of 2006, an estimated eighteen million children were displaced, including both refugees and internally displaced children – which accounts for over half of all displaced people. During flight and displacement, children can become separated from their families, further exposing them to exploitation. Children are disproportionately affected by war in a second way, too. Vulnerable to coercion and forcible recruitment, especially when they are displaced, some 300,000 children participate in armies and armed groups around the world today.

Child soldiers

The ILO's convention on forced labor includes the prohibition of forced or compulsory recruitment of children for use in armed conflict, and the UN sets eighteen as the minimum age for direct participation in hostilities, as well as for compulsory recruitment by governments and all recruitment into armed groups. Yet children are being used in more than thirty current conflicts. They work as porters, messengers, cooks, informants, spies, and as combatants; the availability of light, small firearms has made it easier for small children, some as young as seven or eight, to engage in combat. Girls are also used as cooks and porters and to provide sexual services within the armed group.

These child soldiers are usually from the poorest families in a society and are often displaced from their homes. Uneducated children and orphans are more prone to recruitment. Many join to escape domestic violence, abuse, or poverty and some respond to political propaganda. Rarely is there genuine voluntary recruitment, with the child having full knowledge of the duties involved and informed consent of a parent. Any attempt to leave is punished with beatings, threats of retaliation against the child's family, or threats of death. And in all current conflicts, some children have been forcibly recruited or abducted. Regionally, Africa has the highest rates of children entering armed groups through force or abduction, followed by Asia, the Americas, then Europe.

Since 2001, children have fought in Afghanistan, Angola, Burma, Burundi, Colombia, the DRC, Ivory Coast, Guinea, India, Indonesia, Iran, Iraq, Israel and the Occupied Palestinian Territories, Indonesia, Liberia, Nepal, Philippines, Russian Federation, Rwanda, Sri Lanka, Somalia, Sudan, and Uganda, among other countries. And while the end of wars in Afghanistan, Angola, and Sierra Leone between 2001 and 2003 meant that 40,000 children were demobilized, another 30,000 entered conflicts in Liberia and Ivory Coast during the same period.

In Colombia, both sides engaged in the conflict have used children: the government-backed AUC uses child soldiers as young as eight as informants, and the left-wing guerrilla groups FARC and ELN together use between 11,000 and 14,000 children. FARC has the largest number of minors, including several thousand under the age of fifteen, and minors constitute up to one-third of some units in both guerrilla groups. By 2004, Colombia ranked fourth in the world for the highest use of child soldiers behind Burma, Liberia, and the DRC.

South American children are often forcibly recruited and in some rural areas of Colombia, families must offer their children to guerilla units in order to avoid harm. Other families flee their homes in order to avoid this forced recruitment, and once displaced, women and children are then vulnerable to trafficking for sexual exploitation. The armed political groups also cross over into Ecuador, Panama, and Venezuela and recruit vulnerable Colombian refugees. Once recruited, the children take part in combat, act as messengers and assassins, perform kitchen work, guard duty, and manual labor, carry out executions, and lay explosives. They are regularly executed for acts of disobedience or for trying to escape, and most are denied contact with their families. Half of all recruits to the armed opposition groups are women and girls, who face pressure to enter relationships with male commanders. They are subject to forced use of contraceptive implants, forced abortion, and rape.

Armed political groups also abduct children in India and Nepal. Since 1996, a Maoist opposition group called the Communist Party of Nepal has been engaged in a "People's War" against Nepal's government, and has forcibly recruited thousands of children. Further east, in the Philippines, three major insurgent groups have fought the military since the 1960s and currently hold among them an estimated 2000 child soldiers. The Communist-oriented New People's Army (NPA) began an intense recruitment of children in the 1990s. It now claims to only recruit minors into non-combat positions, but the US State Department notes that children still comprise up to eighteen percent of the NPA's fighting forces. A second group is the Moro Islamic Liberation Front, which recruits children as young as twelve. Parents volunteer their children, seeing it as an observation of Islamic teaching, and Muslim youth organizations recruit students from schools and colleges. Up to fifteen percent of the group's combatants are under eighteen. Finally, the *Abu Sayyaf* ("Bearer of the Sword"), a Muslim separatist group which appeared in the late 1980s, uses Islamic religion to draw minors into the movement where they are used as combatants, human shields, and hostages. Up to thirty percent of its armed members are now children.

In Sri Lanka, children as young as nine have been abducted and used in combat by a rebel group called the Liberation Tigers of Tamil Eelam (LTTE), who demand a separate state for the Tamil minority in the country's North and East regions. The LTTE used child soldiers throughout the major phase of its civil war with the Sri Lankan government, between 1983 and 2002. Children – most aged fourteen or fifteen and over forty percent girls – were used for massed frontal attacks in major battles, and some between the ages of twelve and fourteen were forced to massacre women and children in rural villages. Children as young as ten were used as assassins and other children became human mine detectors and suicide bombers. In the 1990s up to sixty percent of fighters killed were children.

A ceasefire was implemented in February 2002 and the LTTE committed to ending the recruitment of children. But as of November 2004, UNICEF had documented more than 3500 new cases of underage recruitment, while the LTTE formally released only 1200 children during the same period. In 2007, the UN reported that the LTTE had still not ceased its recruitment of child soldiers. LTTE members visit Tamil homes, inform parents that they must provide a child, and threaten any who resist with eviction, child abduction, and violence. In fact, children are now more likely to be forcibly recruited into service: Tamil families see no reason to give their children to the LTTE now the conflict is over, and so the LTTE resorts to abduction and forcible recruitment. In 1994, one in nineteen child recruits was abducted. In 2004, only one in nineteen was a volunteer. Once recruited, those who try to escape are publicly beaten as a deterrent to other children, and most are allowed no contact with their families.

There are many more child soldiers in Africa, however; an estimated 100,000 children between the ages of seven and eighteen. Frequently abducted, they are then used as porters, spies, messengers, and armed combatants. Girls are sexually exploited within the armed groups and are also sent to the frontlines. Children fight other children in Ivory Coast, where they are forcibly recruited by both the government and its opposition groups, and in Burundi, children as young as ten have been recruited to the government's forces. In Liberia, both the government's armed forces and armed opposition groups used child soldiers throughout the country's fourteen-year civil war. Many were forcibly recruited and some were as young as seven. The war ended in 2003, at which point 21,000 child soldiers needed to be demobilized. This demobilization process took many months to begin and it remains unclear how successfully the former soldiers have been reintegrated into Liberian society.

In the DRC, a five-year war between the Congolese armed forces and dozens of armed groups (including the Rally for Congolese Democracy and the Movement for the Liberation of Congo) ended in December 2002. Both the army and the rebel groups had abducted children for use in the war, many under the age of fifteen, and some 30,000 child soldiers needed demobilizing. But the recruitment and use of child soldiers continued. In late 2003, the forces of several armed groups in the eastern provinces comprised forty percent children, and in 2007 an estimated 6000 children remained as soldiers within the government's army and the rebel groups.

Some of the remaining rebel groups are backed by Uganda. And within Uganda itself, one armed group called the Allied Democratic Forces has forcibly recruited children as guards, laborers, and combatants, while another group, the Lord's Resistance Army (LRA), has been abducting and enslaving children for two decades, to use in its armed rebellion against the Ugandan government. Formed in 1987, the LRA is a self-proclaimed Christian guerrilla army and aims to establish a religious state. It operates in northern Uganda and also in southern Sudan, where its presence was approved by the Sudanese government in response to the Ugandan government's support for a rebel Sudanese group (the Sudan People's Liberation Movement).

The UN estimates that the LRA has abducted 25,000 children in northern Uganda since 1987. Approximately 8400 children were abducted between June 2002 and May 2003 alone. Many of the children have been used as combatants, while others become porters, cooks, and domestic workers. Girls as young as twelve are sexually exploited, becoming "wives" of the commanders as well as fighters. And though the LRA and the Ugandan government signed a truce in August 2006, the peace remains fragile and the LRA continues to forcibly conscript children in southern Sudan for use as combatants. These children carry out raids, beat and kill civilians, abduct other children, and burn houses – table 11 details the experiences of children abducted by the LRA. Children who attempt to escape are punished with beatings or public executions, though of the children who do leave, around eighty percent have escaped, rather than being released or rescued. The few releases by the LRA are due to injury or age.

Table 11 War violence experienced by children and youths abducted by the LRA in Uganda

Witnessed a killing	78%
Tied or locked up	68%
Received a severe beating	63%
Forced to steal or destroy property	58%
Forced to abuse dead bodies	23%
Forced to attack a stranger	22%
Forced to kill a stranger	20%
Forced to kill an opposing soldier in battle	15%
Forced to attack a family member or friend	14%
Forced to kill a family member or friend	8%

Source: SWAY, 2006

The Ugandan government itself recruits a small number of child soldiers, as do the militias it supports. And this government's use of child soldiers, along with the Sudanese government's support of the LRA, points to yet another impact of war: government-sponsored slavery. While the Chinese government uses its prisons as factories during peace (as discussed in chapter five), other governments have turned to slavery as a tactic of war.

Government-sponsored slavery

Around the world, government-backed paramilitaries and militias use children, including in Colombia, Somalia, Zimbabwe, and Sudan. Beginning in 1983, a civil war raged between the National Islamic Government of Sudan and the Sudan People's Liberation Movement (SPLM). The Marxist SPLA opposed Sudan's Islamic government, and by 1985 the government had armed some auxiliary militias, known as *murahaleen*, to attack villages in SPLA-controlled areas of the South. In 1989, the government established a paramilitary, the Popular Defence Forces (PDF), to assist its regular army with the counter insurgency. After that, and through the 1990s, government offensives combined PDF, *murahaleen*, and regular army forces. During these offensives, the PDF would abduct children for use in the conflict, as did the government-supported militias and the SPLM. By 2003, even after peace talks had begun, the SPLA admitted to having 13,500 child soldiers, and by 2004, there remained an estimated 17,000 children within all the government forces, allied militias, and opposition groups.

In January 2005, a peace agreement granted southern Sudan autonomy for six years, followed by a referendum on permanent independence. The agreement specified that all child soldiers should be demobilized, but only 1000 children had been released by 2006. Children remained in the ranks of the Sudanese armed forces and the government-backed militias in 2007, while the SPLM continued to recruit and use children. Other militias that did not sign the peace agreement continue to recruit children in southern Sudan and from refugee populations in Chad. As well, just as this North–South conflict was coming to an end, a conflict in the western region of Darfur began in 2003, between the Sudanese government and a rebel group called the Sudan Liberation Movement, then later another group called the National Redemption Front. Both the government forces and the rebel groups continue to use children in Darfur, with the number of child soldiers running into the thousands.

Throughout the 1990s, government-backed armed militias in Sudan also abducted southern individuals for sexual exploitation and forced labor, mainly from the Dinka and Nuer ethnic communities of northern Bahr El Ghazaland and from the Nuba Mountains. Recruits would raid and burn villages, rape and kill civilians, and take women and children as slaves, along with booty of grain and cattle. One study documents 12,000 abductions from southern Sudan between 1983 and 2002, while NGOs and the UN offer estimates of abductees ranging from 10,000 to 200,000. The slaves were usually moved to large towns in the North on week-long journeys during which the women were repeatedly raped, and then sold to new masters who used them without pay in the agricultural and domestic sectors. Some women were forced into early marriages or prostitution.

The ongoing peace process has slowed these abductions, but they do continue. Both government-backed militias and armed opposition groups abduct women and children for sexual exploitation in southern Sudan and now Darfur, and thousands of women remain enslaved. In this region, slave raiding is an act of terror that happens to have an economic by-product. For the government of Sudan, slave-taking was primarily a weapon against the insurgents, and secondarily a way to reimburse its surrogate soldiers for neutralizing this threat. Had the economic logic of slaveholding driven the act of enslavement, then the individuals with the greatest productive capacity, adult men, would have been captured, not routinely killed.

In Burma, however, the government's use of slaves has an economic function. State-imposed slavery has been widespread in Burma for nearly two decades and now accounts for a vast proportion of the two million victims of state-imposed slavery that exist today in the Asia-Pacific region. In 1990 the National League for Democracy, led by Aung San Su Kyi, won a landslide victory in free elections. Refusing to give up power, the military dictatorship arrested her and declared martial law. Since then, the country has operated as a private business benefiting the generals who run the government. Slaves cut timber, mine, and build roads and infrastructure for military units at gunpoint and for no pay. Many of these slaves come from ethnic and religious minorities, which are targeted by the government in its attempt to curb support for armed ethnic groups. Trafficking has also exploded in Burma since 1990: as they flee the military regime, displaced families, especially women and children, are at risk. Thousands of women have been trafficked into forced prostitution in Thailand, and men, women, and children are also trafficked to China, Bangladesh, Malaysia, South Korea, and Macau for sexual exploitation, domestic service, and forced labor.

The US government has enforced sanctions against the country in response to this slave labor and other human rights abuses, but American industry itself has been accused of condoning the military regime's tactics. One of the regime's recent projects was a natural gas pipeline, built in partnership with the US oil company Unocal Corp., the French oil company Total, and the Thai company PTT

Exploration and Production (which is owned in part by the Thai government). The project used thousands of enslaved workers, who were forced at gunpoint to clear land and build a railway next to the pipeline. In 2004, Unocal settled out of court with fifteen villagers from Burma, who had filed a lawsuit within the US, arguing that the multinational corporation should be held civilly liable for forced labor and other human rights violations perpetrated by the Burmese military that provides security for the pipeline.

The Burmese regime also forcibly recruits child soldiers into its military. Whereas the Sudanese government denies the presence of children in its army (and government-supported militias perform more abductions than the regular army), Burma's regime does not deny or delegate the practice. By 2003 there were 70,000 children in the government's armed forces; some were as young as eleven. The army was forcibly recruiting many more: children accounted for up to forty-five percent of new recruits that year. They are forced to participate in armed conflict and are used for forced labor within the military. By 2004, despite a ceasefire with numerous opposition groups, tens of thousands of children remained in the army and several thousand in armed political groups. They are denied contact with their families and frequently beaten. In 2006, the US State Department noted that the government of Burma refused to cease kidnapping children for military exploitation, in spite of pressure from the UN and the US government.

Environmental destruction and natural disaster

The government's use of child soldiers in Burma is fueled in part by its conflict with rebel groups. And the country's vast military enables further enslavement: in the case of the pipeline project and numerous other instances of forced labor, its military (including some of the 70,000 child soldiers) enforces enslavement for non–combat purposes. But the pipeline project points to yet another element of modern slavery: environmental destruction. In Burma, slavery is also fueled by – and itself fuels – a destruction of the natural environment. Slaves building the government's pipeline destroyed Burma's mountain forests. In turn, villagers displaced by the project are vulnerable to enslavement. Equally, when the government uses slaves for logging, this destroys the teak forests. In turn, money from timber sales goes to support military assaults on ethnic minorities opposed to the destruction of their land. Human rights abuses translate into environmental abuses, and vice versa.

Around the world, environmental and human rights issues are closely linked. Just as they are used across the armed conflicts of a region's political landscape, so slaves are used to destroy the natural landscape of a region. From India to Bangladesh, from Indonesia to Ecuador, Guatemala, and Brazil, slaves are pressed to wreck the environment. Forests are illegally cut, strip mines are carved into protected areas, reefs and coastal environments are destroyed, and it is slaves who do this work. The scars of destruction caused by logging and strip-mining in Brazil, India, and West Africa are visible from space and are tell-tale signs of slavery.

In Amazonian Peru and Brazil, the 2000 small-scale gold mines have turned 125 miles of rain forest into mounds of raw earth and ponds choked with mercury-tainted water and silt. To reach the gold flecks, miners dig up riverbanks and haul tons of soil into troughs where jets of water wash a thick brown and yellow runoff back into the river. This clogs streams and pollutes whatever lies down river, while nothing grows on the barren moonscape that remains after the topsoil and vegetation are gone. Mercury is used to extract the gold, and remains in the air, soil, and water. Slaves also work in open pit mines for gold, diamonds, and other minerals in Ghana, Liberia, and the Congo.

Outside Amazonia, the South American forests are cut and burned to make charcoal. The use of wood charcoal to make iron and steel goes back to the eighteenth century and contributed to the deforestation of Europe. In most countries, coke is used in place of charcoal, but where forests are open to criminal exploitation, charcoal-making is common. Unemployed workers from eastern Brazil are tricked with promises of paid work, and then trapped in charcoal camps far from their homes and the rule of law.

In Sri Lanka, mangrove swamps are ripped up to build hundreds of thousands of acres of shrimp and fish farms, where adults and children are enslaved. The mangrove swamps are ecological "sponges" protecting the coastline from flooding. In the tsunami of December 2004, the areas of Sri Lanka that suffered the greatest loss of life were where natural coastal eco-systems had been ripped up to install fish and shrimp farms. This was especially the case when outlying coral reefs were broken up, thus removing a natural buffer.

Then, in a vicious cycle, the destruction generates more and more slaves. Environmental destruction has the greatest impact on the poor, and is itself a force that drives more families toward enslavement. This cycle of slavery and environmental destruction is evident in India, where dam construction forces farmers from their land without compensation. One dam currently being constructed on the Narmada River will submerge hundreds of villages in the states of Gujarat, Maharashtra, and Madhya Pradesh, and displace between 250,000 and one million people, a disproportionate number of whom will be indigenous people. These small farmers cannot just start farming somewhere else; the surrounding land is already taken. Their only option for survival is a loan, and in rural India this means slavery through debt bondage. Once in bondage, slaveholders will put them to work on land that is "available" in the national forests, or other protected areas. They cut the trees and dig quarries, and more of the natural world is destroyed. This displaces more farmers and the cycle begins again.

In another Indian state, Uttar Pradesh, thousands of slaves work in stone quarries and destroy the environment they live in. The forests are cut down for the minerals underneath, and strip mining speeds up the erosion of any remaining soil. Over many generations, lush woodland has became barren desert. Now, even if the slaves escape, there is no other work for unskilled workers in this impoverished area, and the devastated natural environment offers no way to make a living.

Elsewhere in India, natural disaster, rather than man-made destruction, has increased the number of slaves. Drought, landslides, and flooding all destabilize communities, making displaced individuals vulnerable. In the main cotton-growing Indian states of Andhra Pradesh and Punjab, consecutive years of drought have prompted large-scale migrations to the cities. Ill-informed and destitute, they are easy prey for traffickers. Other trafficked women are from the disaster-prone coastal areas, and following the 2001 earthquake in Gujarat, the number of trafficked children from that region increased.

There is one final piece of connective tissue for these factors of natural disaster, environmental destruction, and armed conflict: human health. A major consequence of armed conflict is death and injury, both for civilians and child soldiers, and in regions like southern Sudan where rape is used as a weapon of war, women suffer from STDs and psychological trauma. A natural disaster destroys livelihoods, hospitals, and clean water supplies. Hurricanes and floods are frequently followed by a proliferation of mosquitoes, and a risk of mosquito-transmitted disease. Meanwhile, slaveholders destroying the natural environment have just as little regard for slaves' bodies and minds. Slaves who work in India's quarries lose not only their lush woodland, but also their health. Accidents caused by explosions or drilling are common, chips of rock cut into their eyes, mineral dust fills their lungs, and tuberculosis, malaria, and silicosis are constant companions. Slaves who make charcoal in Brazil suffer from malaria as well. Without running water, they survive on whatever ground water they can find. They also suffer burns and cuts as they work through the night adjusting the slow controlled burn of wood into charcoal. And slaves in the gold mines of Amazonian Peru and Brazil handle and breath in organic mercury compounds. While there is another method used to refine gold, it is even more dangerous: gold-bearing ore is leached with a cyanide solution.

Again, this is a vicious cycle. Malnourished amid a damaged landscape, their healthcare infrastructure destroyed by war or natural disaster, injured by war violence and so unable to rebuild their farms or businesses, too poor to pay for medicine because armed conflict, natural disaster, or environmentally destructive practices have weakened the national and local economies, ill and injured individuals are vulnerable to traffickers and debt bondage.

But what are the most prevalent diseases associated with slavery and trafficking? Does sexual exploitation have a greater health impact than other forms of slavery? Does slavery do more damage to the health of children? Chapter seven examines modern slavery through the lens of physical and mental health.

7

The suffering of multitudes: modern slavery's health risks and consequences

> All slaves suffer more or less, and multitudes much, in their health and strength.
>
> Theodore Dwight Weld, 1839

Today's slaves endure physical and sexual assault, torture, malnutrition, exhaustion, and forced abortions. This inherent violence of slavery is acknowledged in international and national legislation, which uses terms such as "force" and "serious harm" when describing slavery and trafficking. Many slaves are also exposed to deadly diseases such as HIV/AIDS and tuberculosis, and virtually all slaves suffer a debilitating assault to their emotional and mental health. Many are left suffering with substance abuse problems, depression, and post-traumatic stress disorder after liberation or escape. As the US State Department acknowledged in 2007, slavery "has a devastating impact on individual victims."

The State Department added that this impact extends beyond the level of the individual; slavery and trafficking also undermine "the health, safety and security of all nations." Slavery is a global problem and is inextricably linked to international issues such as the HIV/AIDS pandemic, which flourishes where trafficking for sexual exploitation runs rampant. Recognizing this societal impact, the UN's Trafficking Protocol makes slavery a societal responsibility, asking nations to provide medical, psychological, and social services to rehabilitate victims. In confronting slavery around the world, we are confronting at the same time its numerous associated health risks and consequences – on an individual, national, and global scale.

The health risks of forced prostitution

A large proportion of international trafficking victims are women and girls who are forced into prostitution. They are at risk for acquiring sexually transmitted infections and their resulting diseases, such as HIV and AIDS, human papilloma virus (HPV) and cervical cancer, gonorrhea, chlamydia, syphilis, and pelvic inflammatory disease (PID). They are at risk for unwanted pregnancies, and are compelled to have dangerous illegal abortions. And while very little data exists on women in forced prostitution specifically, various studies have explored the health risks of all prostitution. While bearing in mind that the illicit nature of forced prostitution exposes women to greater levels of risk than non-enslaved sex work (because slaves cannot protect themselves nor access health care in a comparable manner), the data can be extrapolated to assess the health risks of forced prostitution.

Women working in prostitution experience higher rates of disease and death than women who do not sell sex. This increased risk was demonstrated by one study that followed nearly 150

STIs AND PID

Most pelvic inflammatory disease (PID) is caused by sexually transmitted infections (STIs) such as chlamydia and gonorrhea that infect the vagina and cervix and then ascend to the upper female reproductive structures including the uterus, fallopian tubes, and ovaries. Recurrent episodes of PID can lead to scarring of these structures, which predisposes women to infertility, ectopic pregnancies, and chronic pelvic pain. In young women, the developing mucosal surface lining the cervix lacks the protective features that are present in older women and as a result, younger women are particularly vulnerable to STIs and PID. Having sex with multiple partners, during menstruation, and without condoms all increase the likelihood of acquiring STIs and PID.

London-based female prostitutes between 1986 and 2000. During the study period, two women were murdered, two died of AIDS, one died from complications of alcoholic liver disease, and one died of intravenous drug overdose; the resulting mortality rate among this group of women was higher than that of similarly aged women not involved in prostitution. Additionally, more than ninety percent of the women reported having at least one STI and many women had a significantly increased incidence of PID and needed to undergo subsequent medical evaluation for infertility. Nearly ten percent of the women had HPV-induced precancerous lesions of the cervix and almost ten percent had contracted hepatitis B or C, which are viruses that infect the liver and can cause chronic liver disease, permanent liver scarring, and liver cancer. Meanwhile, another recent study demonstrated that almost eighty percent of women in prostitution had experienced at least one act of violence and nearly sixty percent had been raped. Finally, a third study assessing brothel-based sex workers in West Bengal found that the prevalence of HIV infection among those prostitutes who were less than twenty years old was two to three times greater than the prevalence among older prostitutes (thirteen versus five percent, respectively). Together, these studies demonstrate that prostitution is associated with increased violence, STIs and other infectious diseases, and death, and that girls and younger women are more susceptible to contracting HIV than their older counterparts.

HPV AND CERVICAL CANCER

One of the most common STIs in the world, more than thirty types of human papilloma virus (HPV) can be transmitted sexually. Although most HPV infections are cleared by an individual's immune system within a few years of infection, some people will have persistent infection that may predispose them to cancer, most notably cervical cancer. After lung and breast cancer, cervical cancer is the third leading cause of cancer-related death in women worldwide and virtually all cervical cancer is caused by HPV.

The first cases of AIDS were reported in 1981 among five homosexual men who contracted a rare form of pneumonia. Today, approximately thirty-three million people live with HIV, including 2.5 million children under the age of fifteen. Every day, nearly 7000 people become infected with HIV and another 6000 people die from AIDS. The majority of new HIV infections each year throughout the world are caused by unprotected heterosexual intercourse. In 2006, for example, about half of new HIV infections in China and Western Europe were acquired through unprotected sex. In India, Senegal, Indonesia, Papua province, Burma, Latin America, and the Middle East, HIV is predominantly spread through unprotected sex, usually involving women in prostitution. In many countries, the spread of HIV is further exacerbated by injection drug use among women in prostitution.

HIV AND AIDS

The human immune system is comprised of various cells that fight disease, including lymphocytes. When certain lymphocytes are infected with HIV, the cells are destroyed, leaving the immune system impaired. Untreated persistent HIV infection eventually results in acquired immunodeficiency syndrome (AIDS), such that the affected host usually succumbs to overwhelming infection or cancer. The majority of HIV infections are transmitted via sexual contact, and infants can acquire HIV infection when the virus enters their mouth and comes into contact with tonsillar lymphoid tissue as they pass through an infected birth canal or when they drink infected breast milk.

To date, the HIV/AIDS pandemic has generated more than fourteen million orphans, and more than ninety percent of these children live in developing nations, such as sub-Saharan Africa, where their poverty makes them vulnerable to traffickers and slaveholders. And although certain medications have turned HIV infection from a lethal disease into a chronic medical condition throughout developed nations, these treatments are not widely available in underdeveloped areas of the world.

It is here, in these underdeveloped areas, that trafficking for sexual exploitation propagates the HIV epidemic (the sexual abuse of slaves in other forms of bondage also contributes). In South Asia, this is the case both within higher-prevalence nations such as India and in lower-prevalence countries such as Nepal (which are linked to neighboring India through an intricate trafficking web). Two recent studies specifically examined the health risks encountered by the girls and women in forced prostitution. The first study analyzed the case records and medical documentation of 175 females who were enslaved in India for sexual exploitation and rescued between December 2002 and July 2005. The average age of the victims when they entered slavery was seventeen years (ranging from eight to twenty-nine years), but almost two-thirds of them entered slavery before their eighteenth birthdays. They had been rescued from slavery at an average age of nineteen years (ranging from nine to thirty years), had spent an average of sixteen months in a brothel environment, and reported having sex with an average of more than seven clients in a typical day. Nearly twenty-five percent of the victims tested positive for HIV, and a longer duration within the brothel environment was associated with a higher likelihood of infection.

The second study focused on nearly 300 repatriated Nepalese girls and women who had been trafficked into India for sexual exploitation between 1997 and 2002. Almost forty percent of the victims tested positive for HIV, and the prevalence of HIV infection among girls who were trafficked into forced prostitution when they were less than fifteen years old was almost four times greater than among women who were trafficked after the age of eighteen. Almost forty percent of girls who were trafficked before the age of fifteen had been prostituted in multiple brothels, and longer duration within a brothel environment again indicated a higher likelihood of being HIV positive.

The findings suggest the following demographic and epidemiological characteristics of forced prostitution:

1. HIV infection is a significant health risk for women in forced prostitution.

2. A longer duration within the brothel environment increases a female's likelihood of contracting HIV.
3. Most girls and young women enter forced prostitution as adolescents.
4. These girls and young women have a significantly increased risk of acquiring HIV.

South Asia, where these studies took place, has the world's second highest prevalence of HIV infection behind sub-Saharan Africa, as well as the largest proportion of women trafficked into forced prostitution each year. Given this high prevalence of HIV, the South Asian women trapped in forced prostitution who have sex with numerous clients every day encounter a perilously high risk of contracting HIV. A longer duration within hazardous brothel environments contributes to this increased risk. Exacerbating the situation, many male clients prefer not to wear condoms when paying for sex, and slaves are often powerless to negotiate condom use. As Dina, who was enslaved in Cambodia, recalls: "An extra payment to my boss and the client does not wear a condom. If I protest I receive a beating." Even when women are able to insist upon condom use, this usually means a fine from the brothel owner, which further entrenches their debt-bondage situation.

Many forced prostitutes in South Asia are trafficked at a young age because prepubescent and pubertal girls are in high demand by male clients who are afraid of contracting HIV and AIDS when paying for sex. These male clients assume that young girls are virgins and therefore cannot transmit STIs. Also, within some South Asian cultures, men believe that having sex with a virgin will enhance their sexual potency and cure them of any pre-existing STIs, including HIV infection. Brothel owners might therefore pay almost twice as much to traffickers for young girls than for older women. These prepubescent and pubescent girls are then particularly vulnerable to sexual trauma and infection during unprotected intercourse for several biological reasons.

Areas of the mucosal surfaces that line the genital tract of younger females are thinner, less mature and more exposed to trauma and infection. Additionally, the violent nature of forceful penetrative inter-course is especially traumatic to a girl's smaller and more immature vagina and cervix. It induces small tears and abrasions within the vaginal and cervical linings, which in turn increase a girl's susceptibility to invasive infection. And finally, some girls are forced to douche with mild astringent solutions, such as alcohol, to dry the vagina. The douching is intended to make the vagina feel "tighter" for male clients, and the resulting dehydrated vaginal mucosa is more prone to tearing. This increased susceptibility to STIs then confers an increased risk for HIV. Prostituted children who are infected with an STI that causes genital ulcers have a four-fold increased risk of acquiring HIV infection.

For women of all ages, menstruation represents another risk factor in contracting infections. When the uterus bleeds and sheds its endometrial lining, the female genital tract is less resistant to infection. Often, women in forced prostitution must have sex with clients while menstruating, thereby increasing their susceptibility to STIs. Maria, who was trafficked from Mexico into the US, recalls: "We worked no matter what. This included during menstruation." She adds that menstruation also brought with it a different kind of health risk: physi-cal assault if slaves were not able to conceal their menses. "Clients would become enraged if they found out," she explains. "The Bosses instructed us to place a piece of clothing over the lamps to darken the room. This, however, did not protect us from client beatings."

Practices such as having sex while menstruating, douching, and not using condoms, as well as younger females' increased susceptibility to acquiring STIs and the high prevalence of HIV in regions where slavery thrives, all contribute to a substantially increased risk of contracting HIV for women and girls in forced prostitution. These risks are then compounded by their lack of knowledge about HIV and other STIs. Many women and girls in forced prostitution are unfamil-iar with signs of disease, and their brothel managers do not provide appropriate screening or medical care. As Nu, a young Thai woman trafficked into a brothel in Japan, explains, "[w]e didn't know much about STDs and AIDS, except the names of these ailments."

HIV and other STIs are not the only health risks endangering women in forced prostitution. Their particular form of enslavement brings with it the attendant risk of unwanted pregnancy. Young girls are especially vulnerable, as ninety percent of adolescent females who do not or cannot use contraception will become pregnant within one year of continued unprotected sexual intercourse. And among girls aged fifteen to nineteen, pregnancy-related deaths (from complications of obstructed labor, infections, hemorrhage, or unsafe abortions), represent the leading cause of death worldwide.

A large proportion of this morbidity results from unsafe illegal abortions. Although safe methods of abortion, using vacuum aspiration or controlled doses of progesterones, are performed throughout the developed world, most trafficking victims are denied access to these methods because they are in parts of the world where abortion is illegal, or because access to legal abortion is denied by slaveholders who do not want to risk discovery. As Nu explains: "We were only taken to the doctor when we were unable to stand. The owner was afraid that his illegal operations and our illegal status would come to light if we were exposed to outsiders." Consequently, many pregnant slaves experience botched surgeries which threaten their lives and can leave them

UNSAFE ABORTION

The World Health Organization terms unsafe abortion a "preventable pandemic." Twenty million unsafe abortions are performed in the world each year, the overwhelming majority in developing countries. They are responsible for approximately fifteen percent of all maternal deaths in the world each year, killing an estimated 68,000 women annually from complications such as hemorrhage, overwhelming microbial disease, or toxicity from the agents used to induce labor. Additionally, millions of women who undergo unsafe abortion procedures are left with reproductive or abdominal organ damage. This damage predisposes them to chronic infection and pain, infertility, and an increased risk of spontaneous abortions in the future. Numerous methods are utilized to abort an unwanted fetus and include injecting corrosive liquids such as bleach into the vagina and uterus, inserting foreign objects such as knitting needles, chicken bones or sticks dipped in oil into the cervix and uterus, pummeling the abdomen with a fist or blunt object, and forcing a woman to jump from a height.

maimed or infertile. Nu recalls the violent abortion methods employed by two other slaves who became pregnant: "They consumed some medicine and one of them aborted. The other got the girls to stamp on her stomach till she aborted." And Jill, an American woman who was enslaved in forced prostitution as an adolescent, describes a violent abortion inflicted by a slaveholder: "Having been hung from the ceiling by my wrists while my pimp attempted to abort a child that I was pregnant with, I was in shock and nearly unconscious when I was brought into the hospital. A broken, long neck beer bottle had been shoved into my vagina … the abortion attempt nearly killed me."

Physical violence extends beyond forced abortions, as well. It permeates all aspects of forced prostitution, from trafficking through "training" into enslavement. Jill recalls her "training" period as "months of being tortured, starved, dehydrated, sensory deprived and raped." Such violence is deployed to break slaves' sense of independence, to "prepare" them for having sex with numerous partners each day, and to discourage attempts to escape. Then, Jill adds, once the slaveholder was "satisfied that my training period was nearing the end, he began to refer me to 'clients' who would use my body for their fetishes." Clients inflict their own forms of violence: "They would beat us before intercourse with sticks, belts or chains, till we bled," remembers Nu. "There were some clients who inserted coke bottles into the girls' vaginas [or] gave the nipples electric shocks."

From HIV and other STIs to unsafe abortions and pervasive physical violence, the health risks of forced prostitution are extreme – especially for girls and younger women. The high demand for young females also means that they are carefully hidden and frequently moved among numerous brothels, and in turn, this hinders rescue efforts by law enforcement authorities and outreach organizations. Like all forms of slavery, forced prostitution is a hidden health emergency.

The health risks of forced labor slavery

While millions of girls and women are exposed to the health risks of forced prostitution, a greater majority of today's twenty-seven million slaves are exploited in forced labor situations. It garners less media attention than sexual exploitation, yet the health issues of forced labor slavery are no less urgent. As one medical editorialist observes, if "promotion of health in the context of trafficking is to be achieved, then we should work to address difficulties faced by other trafficked people such as domestic servants, workers in the carpet and garment industries ... agricultural laborers and camel jockeys."

Many forced labor slaves come from impoverished communities where untreated communicable diseases are rampant. When those who are trafficked arrive in a country such as the US, they usually have not been immunized or medically screened at the point of entry. In one study, for example, up to forty-seven percent of migrant farm workers on the east and west coast regions of the US tested positive for tuberculosis. A highly contagious disease that can destroy the lungs and disseminate throughout the body to damage other organs, tuberculosis is a leading cause of death throughout the world, killing nearly 1.5 million people in 2005. Contagious diseases such as tuberculosis flourish and spread in slaves' squalid and overcrowded accommodations. Dozens of slaves might be kept in a small and poorly ventilated structure without hot water or toilet paper, and with one toilet and shower for the entire group.

Aside from the contagious diseases they may bring with them into slavery, another hazard facing those trafficked into forced labor is the journey into slavery itself. They are often furtively transported within and across national borders to their work destinations and endure extended periods of time in confined spaces such as shipping containers and packed railcars. These passages are frequently characterized by overcrowding, lack of food, dehydration, poor sanitation, and exposure to environmental extremes such as heat and cold. In April 2008, for example, fifty-four Burmese migrants being trafficked in southern Thailand suffocated in the back of a truck.

Those forced laborers who do not fall ill with infection or perish during the trafficking process engage in agricultural work, chemical and materials manufacturing, commercial fishing, mining for diamonds and other natural resources, loom weaving and other clothing production, and domestic servitude, to name a few industries that use slave labor. They work with dangerous cutting machines and other machines in motion, on construction sites, with wild animals, oxyacetylene blowpipes, heavy weights, and hot metals. The illicit nature of this labor entails a disregard for any occupational health and safety guidelines. As well, the slaves are frequently untrained and work long hours, which increases the likelihood of injury, disability, or death.

For example, slaves are forced to work long hours in agriculture, construction, or manufacturing, where they perform constant, repetitive movements and develop strain injuries such as carpal tunnel syndrome or intractable back pain. When untreated, these ailments can lead to permanent disabilities. Equally, slaves in factories and mines, and those working in charcoal production, are often denied protective equipment such as face masks. Consequently, they inhale particulate material that can cause chronic lung disease, including cancer. Agricultural slaves who are exposed to high levels of organophosphate pesticides can experience numerous ailments ranging from persistent headaches to permanent nerve damage. Deafness and blindness can result from a lack of appropriate ear and eye protection in many work environments, such as loud manufacturing plants and metallurgic facilities, respectively. Children who are forced to carry heavy loads suffer from hernias that are often untreated and can consequently become strangulated and infected. Crush injuries to hands and feet occur among laborers who are forced to carry heavy loads when fatigued, or who work with poorly maintained machinery. Many women in forced labor are often sexually abused by their male owners, and consequently are subjected to sexual health risks.

In the case of child slaves, their small size renders them particularly useful in the mining industry, as they can easily navigate small underground passageways. But these tasks expose them to toxic underground gasses, including carbon monoxide, and small airborne particles that can produce acute and chronic lung disease, including silicosis. These children are also at increased risk of serious physical trauma and death as they tend to labor in mining operations that lack adequate safety precautions. Young boys are in high demand to serve as jockeys in the camel racing industry, as well. The sport is inherently dangerous, and because the stakes involved in wagered betting are often high, the penalties for losing a race are severe – involving food and sleep deprivation and brutal beatings, sometimes to the point of death. Children are also exploited as street beggars in urban centers of developing countries, and in some instances are physically maimed by their captors so that they elicit greater sympathy and therefore more money. And finally, forced child military service has its own associated hazards, most obviously an exposure to the inherent dangers of warfare, including disfiguring injuries and death from small and large ballistics or land mines.

Slaveholders maintain control of these children through the use of violent force. Ashok, a former child slave in India, recalls that when he was not able to finish his work, he "received beatings with a slipper and bamboo sticks from the owner of the factory." One day, he adds, this "torture crossed its limit: both my hands were tied to the trunk of the tree and I was beaten very badly. I was not able to come out of that situation for more than one and a half months." This violence extends to adults too. Some manufacturing plant owners run electric current through the factory tables to periodically shock workers to keep them awake, and other slaveholders maintain order by forcing slaves to work at gunpoint and shooting anyone who attempts to escape.

All these health risks are exacerbated by a lack of sufficient rest and nutrition. Sleep deprivation serves as punishment and a control mechanism, rendering slaves physically unable to resist their bosses or attempt escape. Ying, who was enslaved in a Chinese factory, remembers: "We were allowed very little sleep each day; we were forced to start working the moment we opened our eyes [and] I often worked until midnight. We were not allowed to sleep unless we finished the quota. We were forced to work over 16 hours every day." Food deprivation is equally common. As Ashok observes, "the food was watery with no nutritious value and of such a bad quality that even animals would also not wish to eat it." Malnutrition is especially devastating to child slaves because it impairs their physical and mental development. It leads to nutritional deficiency disorders such as nightblindness, induced by vitamin A deficiency, or scurvy, which results from inadequate vitamin C intake and causes easy bleeding, poor wound healing, and fatigue.

Malnutrition also impairs the immune system's ability to fight infection and to help the body recover from injury. Consequently, children freed from forced labor in Ivory Coast, Haiti, India, and Togo not only demonstrate severe malnourishment but suffer from numerous infections, including untreated parasitic infestations of the skin and intestines, oral fungal infections, viral and bacterial diarrhea, worm infestation, typhoid fever, malaria, and tuberculosis. In fact, malnourishment contributes to one out of every two childhood deaths associated with these and similar infections in developing countries each year. Those slaves who are infected with HIV experience even more profound immune suppression and susceptibility to serious infectious complications, particularly from tuberculosis.

Many sleep-deprived and malnourished slaves who are forced to labor in unregulated and hazardous environments inevitably sustain injuries. They might then be subjected to primitive "medical care" from their bosses, in lieu of appropriate medical attention. One

Figure 13 Rambho Kumar

former child slave in India, Rambho (see figure 13), recalls that when his hand was cut on the carpet loom, "the owner and his brother shut my eyes and put my finger in boiling oil and said: 'Now it's all right, now you get back to work.'" Ravi (see figure 14), another child who was enslaved in a carpet loom in India, recounts that when his fingers bled, the slaveholder's wife "would take a little bit of kerosene and put it in my wound and strike a match to it." He added: "The wound would not heal, and I was made to go back and resume weaving again … With the blood running down my finger I was made to weave." Convalescent care is also frequently withheld when slaves become sick. As Ashok recalls, "at the time of any illness and sickness such as fever, pain in my legs, hand, backbone, I was treated badly and not given any proper care to recover from the sickness." One outcome of these mismanaged or untreated injuries – including carpal tunnel syndrome, back pain, and fractured bones – is that their physical consequences remain with the victims, sometimes leading to permanent disfigurement or disability.

Figure 14 Ravi Shanker Kumar

Slavery's psychological effects

In addition to extreme physical and sexual violence, constant exposure to health risks such as HIV/AIDS and other STIs, a paucity of medical care, sleep and food deprivation, and hazardous and inadequately regulated work conditions, today's slaves also encounter intense emotional and psychological abuse. This includes threats of physical and sexual violence, infantilization, and social and emotional isolation from friends and family. Such tactics are intended to wrest any sense of control from the slaves, rendering them disempowered and entirely dependent upon the slaveholder. When such coercive control is established, enslavement is complete and physical force may no longer be necessary. The slaves are so oppressed by the slaveholders' psychological control that they won't try to escape when taken out in public. Combined with the trauma of physical and sexual assault, this psychological control often inflicts debilitating pathology that remains with former slaves for the rest of their lives. As Jill recalls, years after escaping from forced prostitution, "depression is still part of my life, as is shame, fear and a strong drive for self-destruction … There are extensive and deep scars many places on my body. Emotionally, the effects were worse. Flashbacks, nightmares and depression have been constant battles since my escape."

Former slaves suffer from countless emotional and psychiatric problems, including depression, psychosis, anxiety, eating disorders such as anorexia, and post-traumatic stress disorder (PTSD). The prevalence of psychiatric disorders is much higher than among the general population. One study demonstrated that nearly ninety percent of women trafficked both within their countries and across international borders suffer from severe depression. Individuals such as Jill, who have a "strong drive for self destruction," are also at risk of suicide attempts. In another study, for example, over forty percent of prostituted adolescent girls in the US who had become pregnant reported that they had seriously considered or attempted suicide within the past year. And psychological trauma results in psychosomatic disorders too, in which chronic, intractable pain or constant, nonspecific ailments such as diarrhea or chest pain recur without an identifiable "organic" cause.

Some former slaves suffer from substance abuse problems. In order to cope with their experiences and endure their work, many slaves – and especially those involved in forced prostitution – resort to drugs and alcohol. Nu explains that "we routinely used drugs before sex ... because then we didn't feel the pain that much," and Inez, who was trafficked from Mexico to the US, remembers: "I would get myself drunk before the men arrived, so that I could stand the work ... and then go to bed drunk because it was the only way I could fall asleep." Slaveholders might even forcefully administer psychoactive drugs in order to maintain control; this constant drug use leads to addiction that in turn deepens the slave's level of dependence. If left untreated, such addictions can seriously impair a former slave's ability to respond to rehabilitative efforts.

Another devastating result of severe and repetitive physical and emotional abuse is PTSD – the characteristics of which are described by Jill: "sleep was filled with nightmares, daytime with flashbacks and raging paranoia." Some slaves are diagnosed with a PTSD-variant termed Complex PTSD which acknowledges that there has been a prolonged period of total control exerted over the victim by another person. In one study, nearly seventy percent of prostituted women in nine different countries met the diagnostic criteria for post-traumatic stress disorder. The treatment of PTSD and former slaves' other psychiatric disorders requires committed and regular psychotherapy, sometimes in conjunction with appropriate psychopharmacologic agents. If not treated, these disorders can lead to harmful behaviors such as anorexia. "After three years of eating dog food and being forced to beg for it, I was unaccustomed to eating anything normal and struggled with anorexia," explains Jill. "In essence, I still didn't exist as anything more than a slave, except I was an escaped slave." As former slaves begin the long journey toward recovery – toward becoming what Jill describes as "more than a slave" – their rehabilitation is as much psychological as it is physical.

PTSD

Post-traumatic stress disorder, or PTSD, refers to a mental disorder in which a victim of trauma repeatedly re-experiences the ordeal through nightmares or flashbacks, constantly feels fearful, helpless, or anxious, and avoids anything that recalls the experience. Those experiencing PTSD have high rates of concomitant depression, anxiety, and substance abuse problems, and also suffer from chronic and debilitating illnesses including digestive, musculoskeletal, and neurological disorders and chronic pain. PTSD is more likely to develop in young people and in situations where the traumatic experience repeatedly occurs over an extended period of time in an interpersonal manner (as with forced sexual intercourse).

The forensic response

As they begin rehabilitation and receive psychiatric and psychological care, slaves might undergo thorough forensic medical examinations, both as part of their evaluation and also as part of the evidence-gathering process for prosecuting their traffickers and enslavers. The crimes for which traffickers and slaveholders can be convicted include document theft and destruction, involuntary servitude, kidnapping, forced or compulsory labor, unlawful coercion, physical and sexual assault, and murder. But convictions are difficult to obtain as they necessitate meticulous evidence collection. In the US, Europe, and the UK, governmental organizations continue to evaluate how best to achieve successful convictions. They recognize that prosecution attempts relying solely on witness testimonial are least successful and that other forms of evidence must be gathered for each individual case. As the Chair of the Stability Pact Task Force on Trafficking in Human Beings explained in 2003, pieces of evidence must be "fitted together like a mosaic" to strengthen the witness testimony.

Many of these sources of information are found on and in the bodies of the victims themselves, necessitating the performance of forensic examinations. Forensic medicine refers to the application of medical science to the law and involves gathering and interpreting physical evidence that can subsequently be used in legal proceedings, to either exonerate an innocent suspect or convict a guilty criminal. Forensic pathologists are specially trained physicians who focus on the ways in which disease and injury affect the human body. These experts usually examine the deceased and determine the cause and manner of an individual's death through autopsy and studies that include toxicology and radiology. But there is an increasing demand for pathologists to examine and interpret injuries in living victims. The need for forensic examination of former slaves is acknowledged in the TVPA, which also calls for the development of national protocols on conducting these examinations. As more and more perpetrators begin to be prosecuted, such standardized approaches will be increasingly necessary, especially in cases of torture and sexual assault, which require the highest standards of evidence to obtain a conviction.

Recently, a group of physicians championed the need for forensic medical assessment of slaves. In a 2007 article, they acknowledged the numerous health risks associated with slavery and called for the incorporation of standardized forensic medical examination into current post-slavery care. The authors emphasize that a timely and competent forensic examination is necessary to document both injuries and the extent of physical or psychological impairment in a victim. This documentation is vital to both the State, which will charge the trafficker or slaveholder with various criminal offenses, as well as to the victim, who may wish to pursue civil claims against the perpetrators. As the authors state, "[forensic] examination must be carefully planned and structured to furnish medical corroborative evidence of any injury, infection or illness that may have occurred as a result of the trafficking abuse ... that will be taken into account in the sentencing process."

Various protocols for conducting appropriate forensic examinations of torture and sexual assault victims currently exist, including the UN manual on the effective investigation and documentation of torture and the World Health Organization's guidelines for medico-legal care after sexual violence. The physicians drew upon these resources to offer, more specifically, forensic evaluation guidelines for trafficking victims. Briefly, a thoughtful and considerate forensic examination should only be performed with victims' consent and in a manner that does not re-traumatize them. The procedure itself should involve a thorough physical examination, with particular attention directed to documenting injuries and collecting appropriate fluid and tissue samples for laboratory testing, as well as to noting diseases that can be appropriately treated.

Standardized procedures for collecting this comprehensive information will also help address the paucity of hard data on slavery's myriad health risks and consequences. As the authors conclude, "such analysis is helpful for a better understanding of the health hazards related to trafficking in human beings and the possible development of specific preventive measures and strategies." For governments seeking measures to combat slavery, medical forensics is becoming a vital aspect of their efforts.

Recommendations for healthcare providers and other first responders

The UN's Trafficking Protocol stipulates that it is the responsibility of each state to provide "for the physical, psychological and social recovery of victims of trafficking in persons." In order to provide these services, it is first necessary to identify current slaves so they can be helped to freedom. This means that people must be educated to recognize signs of slavery and to direct slaves toward appropriate social and legal services. Healthcare professionals in the community – especially those who work in emergency rooms serving busy urban areas or in smaller rural health centers caring for large immigrant populations – have a unique opportunity to identify, evaluate and assist trafficking victims and slaves.

These healthcare providers and other "first responders," including social service organizations and law enforcement personnel, require preparation and education. A guide to assessing suspected slaves, which includes potential questions that can be asked, is included in chapter eight of this book. In addition, the US Department of Health and Human Services' "Rescue and Restore Campaign," which has received more than 4000 calls to its hotline since it opened in February 2004, provides valuable information kits for healthcare professionals, social service organizations and law enforcement agencies. It is important, however, that physicians or other first responders who engage suspected trafficking victims or slaves proceed in an appropriate manner that "does no harm" to the victim, and guidelines for interviewing do now exist.

As many victims in the US and UK are adolescent girls, diagnostic, therapeutic, and preventive health services must be developed for those identified as enslaved children. The PREVENT mnemonic offers a helpful strategy for managing the health consequences of child prostitution. PREVENT can be utilized within the community healthcare setting, and can be adapted for use with adult slaves as well.

PREVENT MNEMONIC

Psychological counseling for mental illness, emotional harm, and substance abuse;

Reproductive health services for contraceptives, prenatal care, and safe abortions if desired;

Education on strategies to avoid abuse and violence;

Vaccinations for both prostituted children and their infants;

Early detection of potentially lethal diseases through appropriate screening tests;

Nutritional assessment and counseling;

Treatment of diseases and the provision of preventive health services for infants born to prostituted children.

At the national and international level, healthcare professionals can assist both government agencies and nongovernmental organizations in developing and instituting policies that address slavery's health risks. It is especially crucial that the link between HIV and slavery be clearly established and incorporated into any anti-slavery policy. Certain vulnerability factors, such as poverty, gender discrimination, social marginalization, and lack of education are common to both slavery and the HIV/AIDS pandemic. Ending slavery and curtailing the spread of HIV/AIDS can be better accomplished if the medical and anti-slavery communities work together.

A sensitive approach, however, must be employed in addressing this connection between HIV and slavery in order to avoid exacerbating the stigmatization and discrimination that trafficking victims and slaves face in many parts of the world. This warrants special consideration because many women who return to their communities after enslavement are stigmatized, treated as criminals, and denied access to healthcare. This not only deprives the victims of their right to medical treatment but also removes an opportunity to intervene against the global spread of HIV/AIDS.

Finally, many more studies of slavery's health risks need to be designed, funded, and performed, if the healthcare community and policy makers are to provide effective interventions and services. For example, more research into the increased risk of HIV infection among trafficked girls will bring an enhanced focus on rescuing and protecting this particular demographic from slavery, and more research resources aimed at understanding the health risks of forced labor will help expand public and political attention from its narrow focus on sexual exploitation. Efforts to identify and accurately assess health risks and consequences are often thwarted by slavery's clandestine nature, but healthcare professionals can work with nongovernmental organizations and national and international governments as part of a broader effort to expose slavery's secret world. When not merely "medicalized," health considerations can play a vital role in today's anti-slavery movement. The other elements of that movement, and a blueprint for ending slavery, are outlined in the next and final chapter.

8

To effect its abolition: ending slavery in our lifetimes

> As soon as ever I had arrived thus far in my investigation of the slave trade ... [I] determined that I would never rest till I had effected its abolition.
>
> William Wilberforce, 1789

Slavery is ripe for extinction. By ending it, we can achieve in our lifetimes something that makes landing on the moon seem a minor historical footnote. However, there is no simple solution to stopping slavery in every country or village. Ending slavery in America and the UK will be different to ending slavery in India, Ghana, or Thailand. It is integrated into the local as well as the global economy, and every country will need to build a unique set of responses. Japan, for example, has the resources it needs to eradicate slavery very quickly inside the country, but has an extreme shortage of political will. Poor countries may have the best will in the world, but not enough money to take on the slaveholders.

But around the world, slaves are being liberated. And each time a slave comes to freedom, we learn another lesson about how slavery can end. By understanding the social, cultural, political, economic, and sometimes religious packaging that is wrapped around slavery in different countries, we can adapt general patterns to each unique setting.

The state of the struggle

If there was ever a tipping-point where we might end slavery, it is now. Many of the great obstacles faced by abolitionists of the past have   already been removed. First, the moral argument is already won; every country condemns slavery, and no ethnic majority or powerful religious group argues that slavery is desirable or acceptable. The second advantage for today's abolitionists is that there is no economic argument to be won. The monetary value of slavery in the world economy is very small and slave-based revenues flow to support not national economies or trans-national industries, but small-scale criminal networks. The end of slavery threatens no country's livelihood, and the cost of ending slavery is just a fraction of the amount that freed slaves will pump into economies.

The third great advantage is that there is no legal argument to be won. For the most part, the necessary national and international laws are already on the books. Around the world some of these laws need updating and expanding and some need their penalties increasing, but nowhere on earth is slavery legal. Bringing an end to slavery requires the political will to enforce laws, not campaigns to make new ones. As John Miller explained in 2004, while working as Director of the TIP Office at the US State Department, "our struggle is easier than the one facing the nineteenth-century abolitionists. We do not have to violate laws to help the victims as the early abolitionists did."

The laws against slavery in every country, the lack of any large vested economic interest, and a growing acceptance of human rights, mean slavery can be ended when the public and governments make it a priority. And we might also take heart from the fact that while twenty-seven million is the largest number of individuals ever enslaved at one time, it is the smallest ever proportion of the global population to be in slavery.

The major obstacles to beginning the process of eradication are lack of awareness and lack of resources. Significant portions of the global population do not know or believe that slavery exists, including large numbers of policy makers and law enforcement officials who should be at the front line of response. To combat slavery we need to better understand its scope and disseminate this information. This means, first, a commitment to data collection and analysis. In the US, by early 2008, the CIA, the State Department, the Justice

Department, and other agencies had been collecting and organizing information on slavery for almost ten years – and not sharing it. International agencies such as Interpol and the UN have large-scale trafficking databases that they don't share either. If this problem were a health issue, epidemiologists would be combining every data set available to crack it. But information about slavery has not been shared among agencies or made widely available to the public. As we gather data and test strategies, we need to form networks capable of collective thinking focused on ending slavery. Consensus has to be reached on key elements of analysis and orientation. Anti-slavery groups need to join together and cooperate, forming a wider movement with a shared identity. Successful strategies should be proactively offered to the world as an "open-source" program, and grass-roots movements need to identify organizations and entities that are capable of influencing the wider political and economic determinants of slavery. When slavery is linked to exports and products, they need to join with industry. When international pressure could help tip government policies, they need to work with the UN. And governments need to quantify results. In the US, for example, the government has been handing out money to anti-slavery programs since the passage of the TVPA, but with little accountability. One sure way to determine the success or failure of the current war on slavery is through an independent, structured program of monitoring and regular evaluation.

Beyond knowledge-gathering and networking across agencies and groups, we need a greater awareness among the general public. This would lead to increased pressure on politicians to adequately fund anti-slavery efforts. The US government, for example, spent $200 million in 2006 to fight human trafficking and slavery. Compare that to the $12 billion spent on federal drug enforcement in the same year. With so little spent to fight slavery it is not surprising that detection and conviction rates rarely exceed one percent of the estimated existing slavery cases. Even those parts of the government that do work actively against slavery do so on a shoestring budget. The US Immigration and Customs Enforcement is charged with stopping slave-made goods flowing into the country, but is given very few agents to identify these goods. The agents cannot begin to investigate more than a tiny fraction of possible cases.

Public awareness would also increase pressure on politicians to support a series of steps toward ending slavery. Some of these steps are small. For example, the next Peace Corps appropriation bill in the US Congress could include a line announcing that in the next intake there will be a call for volunteers who want to work on the liberation and reintegration of slaves. Other steps are larger. World Health Organization strategies need to be re-focused through a slavery lens, as do government policies on debt relief, law enforcement, and military cooperation with other countries. Foreign aid should be thought through with an anti-slavery focus, some of it targeting the underlying economic desperation that engenders slavery. Trade policies should reflect the idea that slave-made goods are taboo on the world market, and trade financing could be linked to demonstrable efforts to remove slavery from local as well as international markets. Rich countries should devote the necessary diplomatic and financial resources to make the end of slavery a global priority. Some of these resources should be directed to the global South to support the enforcement of local laws against slavery and the establishment of sustainable lives for ex-slaves.

Building an effective international alliance against slavery requires both local and global action. From local police to the UN, from individual consumers to CEOs, we all have a role to play in ending slavery.

The role of the UN and governments

At the international level, existing patterns of research, policy, diplomacy, and outreach should be transferred to ending slavery. The UN is one of the best possible organizations to fight slavery, and the Security Council, the organization's decision-making body, needs to take the lead. If the five permanent members of the Council (Britain, China, Russia, France, and the US) commit to ending slavery, the UN and its many agencies could lead the way.

First, the Secretary-General should appoint a Special Representative for Slavery and Human Trafficking. The Special Representative should be charged with preparing for a meeting of the Security Council concentrating on modern slavery, and the permanent members should contribute funds and resources to ensure that the Special Representative can really attack slavery worldwide. Second, the Security Council should appoint a committee of experts to review the existing conventions on slavery and recommend how to unify and clarify them, as well as coordinate and improve the UN's programmatic response to slavery. Sometimes the improved response will build on existing mechanisms. For example, the UN could adapt its existing strategy for reducing and then eliminating corruption. In the developing world, police and local governments often need a radical shakeup to get rid of deep-seated corruption. The UN has assembled a good anti-corruption team that gets very little publicity but has been successful in a number of countries.

Finally, just as the UN Security Council sends out weapons inspectors, so it should send out slavery inspectors. Most countries in the world have ratified the various UN anti-slavery conventions, and independent, objective inspectors should be deployed to countries to identify and help correct any loopholes in the enforcement of their own laws and their international commitments. The Security Council should establish a commission to determine how the existing UN inspection mandate could be applied to slavery.

At the government level, each country needs an anti-slavery plan. Brazil shows what can happen when a government takes a stand. In early 2003 the president of Brazil set up a commission to end slavery. Laws were strengthened and more money was given to anti-slavery squads. In 2003, close to 5000 people were rescued from slavery by Special Mobile Inspection Groups; by 2005 another 7000 had been rescued. More than $3 million was given to liberated slaves to help them get back on their feet. A company or person caught using slaves is put on an official "dirty list," and in addition to prosecution and imprisonment, that company or person is excluded from receiving any sort of government permits, grants, loans, or credits.

Since a large proportion of slaves in Brazil work where land is being developed (ranching, deforestation, agriculture, and logging in the Amazon and other remote areas), the denial of government benefits to slave-using companies can drive them out of business.

Every government should build a national plan to end slavery within its borders. They could do this by bringing together all relevant existing government agencies, and appointing an anti-slavery ambassador charged with coordinating their efforts and actively involving the local anti-slavery organizations in their countries that are closest to the problem. The ambassador should be charged with leading the development of a national plan which outlines everything that will be required (including what help will be needed from other countries and groups) to stop all forms of slavery. National leaders must be committed to this plan if it is to be effective. And, of course, the plan needs to be followed up with action. Having a national plan helps focus government agencies' efforts and gives constituents of that country a means of holding their government accountable.

Around the world, each government's plan would include different details. For example, in the US, the plan should include fairness in the visa program. There are blatant inequalities in the award of visas for workers entering the US. A nineteen-year-old French or British girl coming as an *au pair* receives a J-1 visa and with it, monitoring, orientation programs, a guaranteed salary, and money for education. Meanwhile, a nineteen-year-old Cameroonian girl coming for the same job receives the lower-level B-1 visa, and a quick visual inspection at the airport. There is no record made of her US address, no monitoring, no guaranteed salary, nothing to prevent her from becoming enslaved.

Another detail in the US plan should be labor rights. When it was passed in the 1930s, the National Labor Relations Act (NLRA) brought fair working conditions to millions of workers in America. Yet two categories were excluded, largely due to pressure from Southern congressmen: farm workers and domestics. These two groups are still denied the rights enjoyed by all other workers. The provisions and protections of the NLRA should be immediately extended to cover these workers, or else they will continue to be more susceptible to enslavement than other workers in America. Yet another detail should be the elimination of slave labor from government contracts. The federal government must definitively renounce the use of forced labor in its works, and monitor and punish any contractors who directly or through subcontractors use tax dollars to enable human trafficking and slavery. It should set up an independent inspectorate to watch over such contracts, and make those contracts transparent.

But while the details might be different from country to country, all government plans should include at least three elements: education, law enforcement, and rehabilitation. One of the best guards against slavery is education. Many people are enslaved through deception. "Recruiters" hold out the chance of a good job to the economically desperate just long enough to take control of their lives. Women in the brothels of Europe, men in the slums of Brazil, girls in the villages of Northern Thailand, and boys in the carpet looms of India all repeat this story.

Against this deception a little education goes a long way. For example, one organization frees young Nepalese women from brothels in India then arranges for them to visit villages to talk about their experiences. After hearing their stories, the parents who were ready to believe the lies of the recruiter, the girls who once yearned for jobs in the big city, the local elders who were bribed by the con-men, are all less likely to be tricked again. For the girls especially, meeting someone much like themselves who faces the death sentence of AIDS is an awakening.

If education is one key to the fight against slavery, we are hardly taking advantage of its power. The group in Nepal sends out its workers, and the IOM carries out public awareness campaigns for young women in Eastern Europe, but literally millions of people at risk are not being reached. The response to the need for public education is piecemeal and reactive. Great sums are spent developing educational campaigns against teen pregnancy or drug use, but who measures the best way to educate against slavery? Governments need to run advertising and education campaigns against slavery and trafficking in the same way they would confront a public health crisis. Public awareness campaigns aimed at potential victims of enslavement should reflect local cultures and be transmitted in appropriate languages.

Alongside this education effort, governments need better training and more funding for law enforcement. Though laws against slavery exist, they are not enforced, in part because only the smallest fraction of police, in almost every country, has been trained to identify slavery and trafficking. Even in the US, where the government spends more on law enforcement than any other country, only a handful of police departments have anyone assigned to human trafficking and slavery and very few officers have been trained to recognize slaves. If the police in the US and other countries are to be more effective, they need an intense and comprehensive nation-wide training program. Training should include those federal agencies involved in fighting slavery, and it should be planned for other workers that are particularly likely to come into contact with slaves: nurses and other medical staff, public health and labor inspectors, and social workers.

Beyond this training, dedicated anti-slavery enforcement teams should be assembled in countries around the world. Brazil is showing how dedicated anti-slavery teams can radically increase the number of people coming to freedom, and this success is occurring with teams that are ill-equipped, under-powered, under-trained, and relatively unsupported by the legal system. A small expansion of the American "War on Drugs" program to include anti-slavery police could make a world of difference. Each year, the US hands out billions of dollars in funds and equipment to other countries as part of this "War on Drugs." Helicopters, aircraft, four-wheelers, training, and salaries are all supplied for use against drug producers and traffickers. Expanding this program to include anti-slavery police would increase the economic cost of enslaving others and the likelihood of punishment, to the point that slaveholding would cease to be viable.

Governments also need to effectively decriminalize and rehabilitate freed slaves. In many countries, freed slaves are treated as illegal aliens or second-class citizens – kept poor and powerless within an informal apartheid system. In some languages, there is a special and demeaning name for ex-slaves. And as they decriminalize the victims of slavery and trafficking, governments need to provide support. In developed countries, it is the role of governments to provide physical and mental health services, language training, and legal and employment counseling to survivors of slavery, taking into account the special needs of children. Governments don't have to take on all these jobs alone; in the US most of the support given to freed slaves comes through experienced service-providers who receive state funds to run their programs.

For the millions of slaves alive today, emancipation is not enough. While it is true that the process of rehabilitation is not well studied, we know that it is essential to sustained freedom. When bonded laborers have been freed in India but given no support to rebuild their lives, some slide back into slavery. Incredibly, some even return to slavery by choice. On the other hand, anti-slavery groups in India have seen that when children are equipped with skills and education, they return to their villages feeling empowered and committed to ending child slavery. These children often become village leaders. The adults come to rely on them because they may be the only people in the village who can read and write, and because they show no fear in confronting landlords or local police.

The role of non-profits and community-based freedom

The example and influence of a single rehabilitated slave can dramatically alter a whole village. They become agents of change, helping their villages to become slave-proof. And this possibility of altering a whole village points to another important element in the process of ending slavery: community-based freedom. In the developing world, this may be the best strategy of all. Rescuing individual slaves can leave the slave-based businesses intact, but when a whole community drives out the slave-takers and slaveholders, freedom is locked in place. Successful community-based solutions need to be scaled up as much as possible.

The chain of cause and effect that leads to communities being able to throw off slavery often starts with a charity, a foundation, or some other grant-making body. The activists and community workers who provide the seeds for liberation are unlikely to have the

KEY RESOURCES FOR FOSTERING FREEDOM

Reliable funding

Indigenous anti-slavery groups need the same stability that they are helping ex-slave communities to build. This doesn't need to be a huge amount of money, just funding that can be counted on. Liberation can be immediate for individuals, but for communities it often takes time. People in slavery live with a great deal of insecurity. Anti-slavery groups must be reliable in everything they do with the communities they support; they can't run out of money in the middle of a liberation.

Flexibility

Local anti-slavery groups need to respond to the needs of slave communities. To do that, local groups need funders that understand flexibility. Six months into a project, anti-slavery workers might realize that providing healthcare is good, but it is going to take micro-credit to get people out of slavery. The point of an anti-slavery movement is to move, always in the direction of ending slavery. If that means changing course from health care to micro-credit, then the funder that is supporting health care needs to allow a shift in focus and to support the direction not just the detail.

Critical thinking

Overcoming slavery means being able to think critically and forcefully about how to get that job done. We need to improve the relationship between non-profit groups that ask for funding and non-profit groups and foundations (including governments) that supply funding. In the current system it is easy to replicate a culture of patronage. But what is really needed is for anti-slavery workers to identify the crucial blockage on the road to freedom. Big foundations need rules; giving away a lot of money requires them. Our challenge is to find the way to increase the level of understanding and trust between the workers on the ground and the funders in their offices, to the point that they work together and become faster, smarter, lighter, quicker, and more powerful than slaveholders.

resources to meet the expenses needed to get the work done. Given the almost total absence of governmental support for community-based anti-slavery work, it is important to consider the chain that goes from funder to anti-slavery worker to slave. To foster freedom in communities, funders and anti-slavery groups need to work together to achieve three key things: reliable funding, flexibility, and critical thinking.

Once this relationship is established between anti-slavery groups and their funders, grass-roots organizations and local and federal governments need to help provide ex-slaves with the essential ingredients of a sustainable future. If communities of ex-slaves are going to survive in freedom, they need certain guarantees.

SAFEGUARDING FREEDOM

Immediate access to paid work

Ideally this is income the ex-slaves generate themselves, doing jobs they know, rather than handouts. The sooner ex-slaves are working for themselves the sooner the community gains stability. Once paid work is underway, the next step is to diversify income, opening chances for ex-slaves to move into other types of work and broadening the economic base of the community as a whole.

Access to basic services

Having a school means the children stay out of work today and build up human capital for tomorrow. A clinic within a reasonable distance means small illnesses don't become debilitating and simple vaccinations save lives. Access to clean water near the home will add hours of productivity to the lives of ex-slaves who could otherwise spend three or four hours each day hauling water. Planning for freedom has to include an audit of what services exist and which are needed.

Savings

For the poor and vulnerable, assets can be the difference between a problem and a catastrophe. Slavery is often the result of having nothing to fall back on in a crisis, and so sliding into debt bondage. When a family has something in reserve, they have the resilience to bounce when they hit the next bump.

> ### SAFEGUARDING FREEDOM (*cont.*)
>
> **Land**
>
> Building a sustainable community in freedom means sustaining the natural environment as well. Many ex-slaves make it clear that one of the first things they want to do in freedom is clear and plant a garden plot. Nutrition and health can make rapid gains with fresh vegetables and beans, and what is not eaten adds to a diversified income. Seeds and a hoe can make a big difference.

The role of industries and consumers

Just as anti-slavery groups, governments, and the UN all have a role to play in ending slavery, so too do industries and consumers. One solution for consumers is to buy Fair Trade products. Within the Fair Trade system, farmers are guaranteed a price for their crops. Once farms have been certified as having no slavery and child labor, and are using environmentally friendly farming methods, farmers can sell their crops to the Fair Trade buyers. The price is not determined by the world market, but is set at an agreed level that will provide a decent life for the farmers and their families. Fair Trade buyers distribute the products to wholesalers and retailers, and currently offer products from more than forty countries, including chocolate, coffee, sugar, and clothing. The supply will increase as more consumers choose to support this way of ensuring a clean product chain. We can buy survivor-made goods, as well. Purchasing products made by survivors of slavery will work towards creating economic empowerment and moving survivors towards self-sufficiency.

We can also use our consumer power to ask companies to examine their supply chains. If companies and consumers work with anti-slavery groups, and everyone takes responsibility for the product chain, then slavery can be removed from the product at its source. The special challenge is to take the slavery out of the products without hurting the free farmers and workers at the same time. Boycotts are not the answer. Western boycotts of certain products can make things worse by hurting the majority of farmers who don't use slaves, even pushing the families of honest farmers into the destitution that makes them vulnerable to enslavement.

For example, in countries in Asia and Africa there may be two cotton farmers out of a hundred who use slaves. If consumers boycott cotton from India or Africa, then the farmers who don't use slaves, who make lower profits, will be the hardest hit by the boycott. They may lose their farms, their children will have to leave school to find work, and their families face debt bondage slavery. Meanwhile, the farmers who use slaves will be better able to survive the boycott since they have been making bigger profits, and they have another resource to fall back on: their slaves, who can be put to work at other jobs (denying those jobs to free workers) or even sold. The boycott may hurt the slaveholder, but it will hurt the free farmer much more.

Instead, anti-slavery activists propose that the best approach is to fight slavery where it is actually happening. That means stopping slavery on the farm, in the mine, or in the workshop. To do that, everyone along the supply chain, from the farmer to the consumer, takes responsibility. A cotton t-shirt, for example, goes through many steps before it reaches the shop: harvested cotton goes from the farm to a cotton buyer; then to a cotton gin; raw cotton from the gin goes to a factory to be spun into thread; the thread goes to another factory to be woven into cloth; and the cloth is then shipped to be made into clothing. After the clothing is packaged, it is shipped to wholesalers; the wholesalers sell it to retailers; the retailers send it to shops where consumers buy it and take it home. Many of the steps along this supply chain take place in different countries, depending on where the t-shirt company and its subcontractors locate their factories.

Everyone at every step along the chain can decide that they won't allow slavery in their product. If they agree to work together it becomes much easier to send anti-slavery workers to the farms or garment factories where the slaves are being exploited. The Cocoa Protocol, described in chapter three, has shown that an industry working together with human rights groups, consumer groups, and labor unions might be able to remove slavery from the products we buy. Another example is the C.F. Martin Guitar Company, which has been working with environmental groups to ensure that the mahogany it needs for top-end guitars is harvested in a slave-free and sustainable way. Slaves are used for logging in the forests of Brazil, Peru, and other South American countries, and the company has been clear that it wants to do whatever it can to clean up its supply chain. It understands the problem has to be solved in the logging camp.

Another good example of business involvement is the Rugmark Foundation, an international charity established in 1994 that inspects and licenses carpet looms in South Asia. When carpet makers apply for a Rugmark license, they promise not to employ children under fourteen years of age in the production of carpets and to pay adult weavers a minimum wage. In family carpet businesses, regular school attendance is required for children employed as helpers and only the loom-owner's children are permitted to work.

Carpet makers also promise to allow Rugmark's inspectors to examine their looms and workers at any time. The inspectors carry out random checks to see that the rules are being followed. If they meet these requirements, a license permits the carpet makers to put a Rugmark label, with a unique serial number, on their carpets so that every carpet can be traced all the way back to the loom where it was woven. Companies that import carpets to Europe and America pay about one percent of the cost of the carpet to Rugmark. This money supports schools and rehabilitation programs for children who have been freed from slavery in the carpet industry. In this way the former child slaves are safeguarded against being caught and enslaved again. Since 1995, Rugmark has certified more than 5.5 million carpets as slave-free, and, as of 2006, Rugmark inspectors had liberated more than 3000 children in India and Nepal.

This model needs to be fostered and extended to other industries whose products are tainted with slavery: sugar, cotton and clothing, fish and shrimp, iron and steel, wood, electronics, and many others. Governments can act as matchmakers between competing businesses and the anti-slavery movement in this process, and should actively bring together stakeholders who will take on and clean up supply chains. And governments can further help industry to remove slavery from our products. For example, the US has a law that provides for the seizure of suspicious, or "hot," goods, but only if they were made within the country. This means that if the Customs Service does not catch slave-made goods at the border, there is no second chance. The "hot goods" seizure law should be immediately extended to encompass all slave-made goods, regardless of the place of origin, so that they can be stopped and confiscated before they reach our homes.

The role of the individual

Is there anything else the individual can do, beyond challenging industry to remove slavery from the supply chain? The answer is yes. While ending slavery means acting locally and globally, it means individual action, too, and there are steps that we can all take.

We can refuse to retire on the backs of slaves. If you have a retirement fund, tell your investment or pension adviser that you do not want to profit from slavery. Ask that they not invest your money in companies that refuse to take responsibility for the slavery in their supply chains.

You can write to your Member of Parliament or Congressperson. Politicians tend not to respond to an issue without pressure from their constituency. Write or email your government representatives. Don't assume they are familiar with the issue; tell them what you think they should know and encourage them to act. You might also write an OpEd column, or a letter to a newspaper or magazine, or start a blog.

We can all watch for signs of slavery in our communities. A domestic worker, a farm worker, someone in a shop, restaurant, factory, or someone in prostitution is likely to be enslaved if he or she:

- is not free to change employers
- has been assaulted or threatened for refusing to work

- has been cheated and forced to pay off "debts" upon arrival in the US or the UK
- has had his or her passport or other documents taken away
- lacks proper identification
- is unable to move freely or is being watched or followed
- is under the control or constant supervision of another
- is rarely allowed to speak freely
- has an "interpreter" with them
- lacks the means to support him/herself or control money, in spite of long hours at work
- lacks contact with or is isolated from family and friends
- lacks permanency in the community
- has a constant appearance of fear, nervousness, and/or apprehension
- is afraid to talk in the presence of others
- has unexplained injuries or is malnourished

There are many clues that a person is a slave. Some, such as confiscation of passports, debt bondage, and lack of control over earnings, tend to be revealed only during the course of careful investigation by victim advocates, service providers, and trained and sensitive police officers. Any of us, however, can pick up on other signs of enslavement. One is the presence of trauma – injuries, bruising – that might indicate a pattern of physical abuse. Untreated infections can also be a sign that a person is enslaved. Another possible indicator is a person's demeanor. Does he or she appear fearful, reluctant to communicate, or generally withdrawn? A slave has been programmed to fear outside contact. He or she is likely to believe that the police are cruel and corrupt, and that any connection with the outside world could result in jail or deportation. In many instances, the slaveholder has warned the victim that an attempt to escape or communicate with the authorities will mean injury or death to the victim's family. In addition, slaves may be unable to answer very simple questions because of their isolation. They may not know what city they are in, their street address, or their phone number.

Slavery often comes to light because a member of the public sees something odd and speaks up. You could ask:

- Can you leave your job or situation if you want to?
- Can you come and go as you please?
- Have you been threatened for trying to leave?
- Have you been physically harmed in any way?
- What are your working or living conditions like?
- Where do you sleep and eat?
- Do you sleep in a bed, on a cot, or on the floor?
- Have you ever been deprived of food, water, sleep, or medical care?
- Do you have to ask permission to eat, sleep, or go to the bathroom?
- Are there locks on your doors or windows so you cannot get out?
- Has anyone threatened your family?
- Has your identification or documentation been taken from you?
- Is anyone forcing you to do anything that you do not want to do?

Bus stations, train stations, and service stations are logical places to look for slaves. Traffickers that exploit women in forced prostitution frequently transport their "girls" from city to city to avoid discovery. Some of them sell their victims' services at train and bus stations and others are just passing through. And, since the vans transporting victims have to stop for gas, service stations are natural stop-offs for traffickers. Station attendants can look for large numbers of fearful people being guarded as they use the restrooms. These same restrooms are good places to display information, in several languages, offering immediate help to victims, in the form of the telephone numbers for local NGOs, police, and trafficking hotlines. Equally, anyone working in a hospital should be aware that a third party insisting on interpreting, or being present for conversations with a patient, is a sign of control that can indicate enslavement. The same is true if a person seems to be "guarded" by someone else when visiting hospitals or clinics. The fact that a trafficker or slaveholder brings in a victim for medical attention doesn't imply concern for the person's welfare; it could simply be motivated by the possibility of lost revenue.

One of the most insidious forms of slavery occurs right under everyone's noses: the enslavement of domestics and nannies. Enslaved domestics will have many of the warning signs: someone else holds their documents, and their movement and communication is restricted and controlled. Sometimes a neighbor will become aware that one person who lives nearby is only glimpsed occasionally and never seems to leave with the building's other residents. Individuals might consider joining or creating a Neighborhood Watch to better spot these signs of slavery. If there are already Neighborhood Watch groups in your community, make sure that slavery is included in their agenda. You can meet regularly, stay up to date on all slavery-related issues and developments, and create strategies for monitoring possible cases of slavery within the community. And you can arrange with local schools, colleges, and community centers to sponsor speakers who are professionals in the anti-slavery field.

You could get creative and design your own program. For example, a group of women in Florida are concentrating their efforts on feminine products. They are writing letters to the makers of Tampax, encouraging them to put an emergency hotline message on their packaging. This will let women know – in different languages – that if they're being held against their will, there is a twenty-four-hour number they can call. The Florida women say they chose feminine products because women of all backgrounds and languages use them, and they use them in private, away from the eyes of their captors. Another example is a teacher who helped a group of fifty schoolchildren in Kentucky to fund the rescue and rehabilitation of dozens of trafficked children abroad. As part of their service project, the students learned how to design a website, and to create brochures and slide shows on slavery to educate other students, business leaders, and faith congregations. They also donated baby-sitting money and allowances, baked cookies, and sold lemonade. In six weeks, they raised over $28,000.

Everyone has skills to offer the anti-slavery movement. If you are skilled at organization, then you might consider bringing the idea of a slave-free city to your community. The process of slave-proofing a city may begin when someone raises the idea in a school, in a letter to the local newspaper, or in his or her place of worship. When there is even a small group of people committed to ending slavery, they can find out which existing service providers (sometimes a shelter specifically for survivors of slavery, alternatively, homeless shelters, women's shelters, and immigrant service organizations) are already equipped to help. They can learn about their work, and how they can best be supported. Local foundations can contribute leadership gifts and faith communities and clubs can hold fundraisers for the local social service provision groups.

Public awareness-raising can include articles in the local newspaper, reports on TV and radio, a proclamation by the city government, and special assemblies in schools. A committee, including members of the city council and local business leaders, can examine whether goods sold in the community have a high likelihood of being slave-made. And together with the existing service providers, the group can communicate its vision of a slave-free city with the City Council, the mayor, the police chief, religious leaders, teachers, the Boy Scouts, and the editors and managers of local newspapers, radio, and TV stations. Every one of these community leaders, and others, will need an explanation of the plan to rid the community of slavery.

As many victims come from abroad, and enter the country with little or no capacity to speak English, language is a major issue. The ability to speak, read, and write English is important for survivors seeking to make a life in the UK or the US. If you have a language skill, talk to your local service provider about acting as an interpreter for intake interviews with the staff attorney or legal director. Or you could help anti-slavery and anti-trafficking organizations translate materials so that they can reach a greater number of people in slavery. If you can teach, consider teaching English as a second language to ex-slaves; the service provider may be able to set up classes or tutorials for you.

The cost of ending slavery

Around the world today, slave liberators are like emergency aid workers fighting an epidemic. We can make sure they have the tools they need by giving our time, effort, and money. For every epidemic, research is needed, health policies have to change, the whole public health system of sewers, water treatment, and hospitals has to be re-built. But someone needs to deliver the vaccine and the food *today*. And today there are slaves waiting to be freed. The organizations that liberate slaves know how to set slaves free and they know how to help freed slaves achieve autonomous lives and dignity. What they cannot do is mobilize funds that will help extend their work further.

Small-scale programs for liberation and rehabilitation, in a number of countries, have demonstrated that slavery can be eradicated from communities and regions at a relatively low cost. For example, debt bondage slavery in South Asia accounts for as many as ten million of the world's slaves. If we can crack this form of slavery, millions of slaves will come to freedom. Programs for liberation and reintegration in Northern India are well developed and well tested. The total cost of bringing a family to freedom is around $130 – which includes paying outreach workers, funding their transportation to rural villages, organizing and guaranteeing seed money, maintaining micro-credit unions, and running the local organization's office. In Ghana, the cost of liberating and rehabilitating a group of child slaves from the fishing industry is about $400 per child.

Based on analysis of anti-slavery projects, an estimated cost of the enforcement and rehabilitation programs needed to eradicate slavery around the world is about $15 billion over a twenty-five-year period. Knowing what it will cost to end slavery in a country makes it possible to build an effective strategy for eradication with meaningful government participation. And while individuals can help slave liberators now, there is also a relatively painless way that governments can pay for the larger picture of a slave-free world: debt forgiveness.

European countries have made tremendous progress in debt forgiveness, removing the old debts whose servicing costs were bleeding poor countries dry. Since 1996 the Heavily Indebted Poor Country (HIPC) Initiative, under which rich countries agreed to cancel $110 billion in debt, has removed about $30 billion of debt in twenty-seven countries. This releases funds for real development.

Tanzania has used about $80 million a year that otherwise would have serviced its debt to increase spending on schools and public education. Close to two million children are reported to have returned to school because of the debt relief.

On the other hand, many countries in the developing world continue to carry a significant amount of external or foreign debt to international banks and institutions such as the International Monetary Fund. For example, in 2006 Brazil's foreign debt equaled about $200 billion. Some of that debt is "overhang," loans contracted by the military dictatorship that controlled the country from 1964 to 1985. The Brazilian economy is relatively healthy but the country continues to have a deep divide between its rich and poor citizens, with many of the poor living in absolute destitution – a common contributing factor to enslavement. The debt Brazil services every year accounts for millions of dollars that could be spent on important programs to further stimulate the economy, such education.

So here is a simple first step: the US and the international banks should agree with the Brazilian and other governments that a portion of their debts is to be forgiven, on the condition that a percentage of the money that would have gone to debt service is applied, instead, to eradicating slavery. The cancellation of just $500 million to $1 billion in debt in a country like Brazil would free up significant funds for ending slavery. We already know that debt cancellation can save lives; it could also free slaves. And money spent on ending slavery is an investment, not a donation. Freed slaves know how to work, and they will quickly begin to build assets. They will also become what they have never been allowed to be – consumers who buy food, clothing, and education for their children. In areas with extensive slavery, liberation leads to economic growth. Stable and sustainable freedom will pay for itself.

Looking backward, moving forward

Cut away the disguises and the facts are simple: one person controls another through violence. Penetrate that violent control and the slave becomes free. Help that slave gain autonomy and he or she remains free. And whether it is carrying one slave child to freedom, or crafting policies that free thousands, we have examples before us. Slaves have been coming to freedom for hundreds of years.

In fact, while there are differences between nineteenth-century chattel slavery and the new slavery of the global economy, history does inspire the modern debate. "When one takes on a challenge of modern day slavery, one benefits from the work of others, past and present," explained John Miller in March 2003. Pointing to William Wilberforce, William Lloyd Garrison, and the Underground Railroad, he concluded: "This struggle will not be short or easy. Wilberforce only succeeded in abolishing the nineteenth century slave trade after over 25 years. We will need his spirit and the spirit of our own nineteenth century abolitionists if we are to defeat this modern scourge." The following year, in August 2004, Miller continued his theme. "The struggle will be a long one," he acknowledged. "But so was the struggle … of the American abolitionists like Frederick Douglass and Harriet Beecher Stowe … We need their dedication and energy and patience." The memory of "our abolitionist forebears," he added, could be "a source of inspiration … for those who join the new abolitionist movement."

Today the world is inaugurating that new abolitionist movement. Though still in its infancy, it has made remarkable progress. During bicentennial celebrations of the 1807 and 1808 acts that abolished the British and American slave trades, officials not only looked to the past for inspiration but also acknowledged history's unfinished work. As the UN Secretary General Kofi Annan put it in December 2006: "the two-hundredth anniversary of the abolition of the slave trade in the British colonies … will be a powerful reminder of centuries of struggle and progress in combating slavery – but also of the fact that we still have not managed to eliminate it completely … We must carry on the struggle … Let us pledge to draw on the lessons of history to free our fellow human beings from slavery." And in 2008, Miller was still summoning the memory of earlier abolitionists – asking, like Annan, that we finish their work. "We need hundreds of Wilberforces in more than a hundred countries to finish the abolitionist revolution," he explained. Two hundred years ago, the British Parliament and the American Congress outlawed the trans-Atlantic slave trade; now we might come together again in a global abolitionist movement and complete that work.

Amid celebrations of liberty in 1852, Frederick Douglass asked his audience the meaning of their commemoration: "What, to the American slave, is your Fourth of July?" Today we can adapt his question: what to the modern slave is this bicentennial? And we have the chance to answer that the meaning of the bicentennial is the final – the irrevocable – end of slavery.

Notes

Chapter 1

p. 1 "your nation ... more intolerable": Frederick Douglass, "What to the Slave is the Fourth of July?" in Philip Foner and Yuval Taylor (eds.), *Frederick Douglass: Selected Speeches and Writings* (Chicago: Lawrence Hill Books, 1999), 188–206 (189, 196, 194).

p. 2 Twenty-seven million: Kevin Bales, *Disposable People: New Slavery in the Global Economy* (Berkeley: University of California Press, 1999), 8. This number combines evidence and data from original field research, the United Nations (UN), the International Labour Organisation (ILO), the US Department of State (USDS), and numerous studies by human rights organizations, anthropologists, and economists. It is smaller than the estimates put forward by some activists, which range as high as 200 million.

p. 4 "With little exception ...": M. I. Finley, quoted in Milton Meltzer, *Slavery: A World History* (New York: Da Capo Press, 1993), 69.

p. 5 "[Ham] became a slave ...": David M. Goldenberg, *The Curse of Ham: Race and Slavery in Early Judaism, Christianity, and Islam* (Princeton: Princeton University Press, 2003), 173.

p. 5 "They do not have slaves to wait ...": Peter Garnsey, *Ideas of Slavery from Aristotle to Augustine* (Cambridge: Cambridge University Press, 1996), 78.

p. 6 between 11 and 28 million: David Eltis, *Economic Growth and the Ending of the Transatlantic Slave Trade* (Oxford: Oxford University Press, 1987), 319.

p. 7 "closeness of the place ...": Angelo Costanzo (ed.), *The Interesting Narrative of Life of Olaudah Equiano* (1789, Peterborough: Broadview Press, 2001), 72–3.

p. 11 "a lady with her pen ...": *Frederick Douglass' Paper*, 31 December 1852, reporting speech given on 14 December.

p. 13 "as many as one-third ...": Jacqueline Jones, *The Dispossessed: America's*

Underclasses from the Civil War to the Present (New York: Basic, 1992), 107.

p. 15 By the first decades ... run by Europeans: Gabriel Baer, *Studies in the Social History of Modern Egypt* (Chicago: University of Chicago Press, 1969), 165, 167.

p. 15 In the Soviet Union ... until the 1960s: Anne Applebaum, *Gulag: A History of the Soviet Camps* (London: Penguin, 2003).

p. 15 at the height of the Nazi regime ... munitions and construction: Michael Thad Allen, *The Business of Genocide: The SS, Slave Labor, and Concentration Camps* (Chapel Hill: University of North Carolina Press, 2002).

p. 15 the Japanese military enslaved ... occupied by the Japanese military: Toshiyuki Tanaka, *Japan's Comfort Women: Sexual Slavery and Prostitution During World War II and the US Occupation* (New York: Routledge, 2002).

pp. 18–19 Fifteen to twenty million ... at least ten million: Anti-Slavery International (ASI), "Bonded Labour: the Gap Between Illusion and Reality" (London: ASI, 1997).

p. 19 Eighty percent ... military groups: ILO, "A Global Alliance Against Forced Labour" (Geneva: ILO, 2005), 2.

p. 19 Ninety percent ... ten percent ... seventy-five percent: Ibid.

p. 20 The ILO estimates ... sexual exploitation and domestic service: Frank Hagemann, "Every Child Counts: New Global Estimates on Child Labour" (Geneva: ILO, 2002), 10, 26, 35, 25.

p. 20 Within the number of 8.4 million ... easy prey: Giuseppe Calandruccio, "A Review of Recent Research on Human Trafficking in the Middle East," in Frank Laczko and Elzbieta Gozdziak (eds.), *Data and Research on Human Trafficking: A Global Survey* (Geneva: International Organisation for Migration [IOM], 2005), 267–99 (280); Chris Beyrer, "Global Child Trafficking," *Lancet* 364 (2004): 16–18; UN Commission on Human Rights, "Trafficking and Forced Labour of Children in the United Arab Emirates" (Geneva: UN, 2004).

p. 21 they work more than ... sexually exploited: Hagemann, 10; National Coalition for Haitian Rights (NCHR), "Restavec No More: Eliminating Child Slavery in Haiti" (New York: NCHR, 2002); June Kane, "Helping Hands or Shackled Lives? Understanding Child Domestic Labour and Responses to It" (Geneva: ILO, 2004), 15; UNICEF, "Child Alert: Haiti" (New York: UNICEF, 2006), 3.

p. 21 500,000 children: US Department of Labor, "By the Sweat and Toil of Children, vol. 2" (Washington, DC: Department of Labor, 1995), 85.

p. 21 300,000 children: Bureau of Democracy, Human Rights, and Labor (DRL), "Country Reports on Human Rights Practices: India" (Washington, DC: USDS, 2002).

pp. 21–22 Another hot-spot … sexually abused: Ginny Baumann, "Eradicating Child Slavery in West Africa: Priorities Emerging From Our Work in Ghana" (Washington, DC: Free the Slaves [FTS], 2007).

p. 22 10,000 women and 4000 children … currently 4000 women: Home Office and Scottish Executive, "UK Action Plan on Tackling Human Trafficking" (London: Home Office and Scottish Executive, 2007), 14–15.

p. 22 Many victims continue to be removed … : ASI, "Trafficking for Forced Labour: UK Country Report" (London: ASI, 2006).

p. 22 40,000: Determining the exact number of victims in the US has proven difficult given the hidden nature of forced labor and the government's practice of not counting the actual number of persons trafficked or caught in a situation of forced labor in a given year. Instead, it counts only survivors (defined by the 2000 Trafficking Act as victims of a "severe form of trafficking") who have been assisted in accessing immigration benefits. But multiplying the number flowing into the country by the average number of years spent in slavery provides a conservative estimate of around 40,000 people at any one time.

p. 22 14,000–17,500: Office to Monitor and Combat Trafficking in Persons (TIP), "Trafficking in Persons Report" (Washington, DC: USDS, 2004), 23. Government estimates of the annual numbers of victims trafficked into the US annually have varied and been revised downward. See for example Amy O'Neill Richard, "International Trafficking in Women to the United States: A Contemporary Manifestation of Slavery and Organized Crime" (Washington, DC: Center for the Study of Intelligence, 1999), which states that "an estimated 45,000 to 50,000 women and children are trafficked annually to the United States." In August 2003 the US government noted that "18,000–20,000 are trafficked annually into the United States." See US Department of Justice (USDJ) et al., "Assessment of US Activities to Combat Trafficking in Persons" (Washington, DC: USDJ, 2003), 3.

p. 23 Table 1 data: FTS and the Human Rights Center (HRC), University of California, Berkeley, "Hidden Slaves: Forced Labor in the United States" (Washington, DC: FTS, 2004), 1, 14.

p. 23 up to 7000 come from East Asia … or ethnic background: FTS and HRC, 15.

p. 23 Mexico accounts for the majority … : USDJ et al., "Assessment of US Government Activities to Combat Trafficking in Persons" (Washington, DC: USDJ, 2004).

p. 23 131 cases … 20,000 men, women, and children … ninety US cities: FTS and HRC, 10, 11, 57.

Chapter 2

p. 26 Quotations from Salma and Ramphal: Kevin Bales and Zoe Trodd, eds., *To Plead Our Own Cause: Personal Stories by Today's Slaves* (Ithaca: Cornell University Press, 2008), 222, 230.

p. 34 the following typology … : Patrick Belser, "Forced Labour and Human Trafficking: Estimating the Profits" (Geneva: ILO, 2005), 3. See also Kanchana Ruwanpura and Pallavi Rai, "Forced Labour: Definitions, Indicators and Measurement" (Geneva: ILO, 2004).

p. 35 indicators of forced labor … : ILO, "Human Trafficking and Forced Labour Exploitation: Guidelines for Legislators and Law Enforcement" (Geneva: ILO, 2004).

p. 35 two and half million people … seventy-five percent … twenty percent: ILO (2005), 2.

p. 36 800,000 men, women and children: TIP, "Trafficking in Persons Report" (Washington, DC: USDS, 2007), 8.

p. 36 third largest source: Congressional Research Service, "Trafficking in Women and Children: The US and International Response" (Washington, DC: Library of Congress, 2002), 1.

p. 37 Figure 4: UN Office on Drugs and Crime (UNODC), "Trafficking in Persons: Global Patterns" (Geneva: UN, 2006), 17.

p. 39 of the estimated 200,000 people … 90 percent is inter-state: DRL, "Country Reports on Human Rights Practices: India" (Washington, DC: USDS, 2005); Asian Development Bank (ADB), "Combating Trafficking of Women and Children in South Asia" (Manila: ADB, 2003), 33.

p. 38 up to 200,000 children: Mike Dottridge, "Trafficking in Children in West and Central Africa," *Gender and Development* 10.1 (2002): 38–49.

p. 40 confusion over the difference between smuggling and trafficking: For the debate over whether human trafficking is an immigration issue or a human rights concern, see Wendy Young and Diana Quick, "Combating Trafficking in the UK," *Forced Migration Review* 25 (2006): 41, and Beth Herzfeld et al., "Trafficking: Immigration or Human Rights Concern?" *Forced Migration Review* 25 (2006): 39.

p. 41 116 people ... 111 people: TIP, "Trafficking in Persons Report" (Washington, DC: USDS, 2006), 49; TIP (2007), 53.

pp. 44–5 Tables 5 and 6: Belser, 17.

Chapter 3

p. 48 "underside of globalization": ILO (2005), 5.

p. 56 "Extreme poverty means ...": Jeffrey Sachs, *The End of Poverty* (New York: Penguin, 2005), 21.

p. 58 "must use its limited tax revenue ...": Ibid., 59.

p. 60 "tolerant" of organized crime: David Johnson, "Above the Law? Police Integrity in Japan," *Social Science Japan Journal* 6 (2003): 19–37.

p. 60 "policemen return women ...": Kaname Tsutsumi and Sumiko Honda, "Trafficking in Persons from the Latin American and Caribbean (LAC) Region to Japan" (Washington, DC: Organization of American States, 2005), 28.

p. 62 Robert B. Smith, "Global Human Development: Explaining Its Regional Variations," unpublished paper, September 2006, 10.

Chapter 4

pp. 65–6 Quotations from Kaew, Nu, and Dina: Bales and Trodd, 90, 97, 91, 103.

p. 66 half of international trafficking cases: TIP (2007), 8.

p. 66 fifty-six percent ... ninety-eight percent: ILO (2005), 2.

p. 66 800 and 1200 people: J. Oxman-Martinez et al., "Victims of Trafficking in Persons: Perspectives from the Canadian Community Service Sector" (Ottawa: Research and Statistics Division, Department of Justice Canada, 2005), 2.

p. 66 seventy-five percent of them were women and girls: A. Kapoor, "A Scoping Project on Child Trafficking in the UK" (London: Child Exploitation and Online Protection Centre, for the Home Office and Border and Immigration Agency, 2007).

p. 66 eighty percent ... seventy percent: USDJ (2003), 2–3; See also Janice Raymond and Donna Hughes, *Sex Trafficking of Women in the United States: International and Domestic Trends* (Amherst: CATW, 2001).

p. 67 100,000 to 500,000: Malika Floor, "UNHCR's Role in Combating Human Trafficking in Europe," *Forced Migration Review* 25 (2006): 23–4.

p. 67 fastest-growing criminal activity ... ninety percent of non-national women ... over two-thirds of trafficked women: Elizabeth Kelly, "Journeys of Jeopardy: A Review of Research on Trafficking in Women and Children in Europe" (Geneva: IOM, 2002), 26, 29, 19.

p. 67 UN ranks ... as origin countries: UNODC, 26–7.

p. 67 explosion in the export: Donna Hughes, "Trafficking for Sexual Exploitation: The Case of the Russian Federation" (Geneva: IOM, 2002), 5

p. 67 100,000 women: Alja Klopcic, "Trafficking in Human Beings in Transition and Post-Conflict Countries," *Human Security Perspectives* 1.1 (2004): 7–12.

p. 68 in Israel is 3000: Leah Gruenpeter Gold and Nissan Ben Ami, "Evaluation of National Authorities Activities and Actual Facts on the Trafficking in Persons for the Purpose of Prostitution in Israel" (Geneva: UN, 2004), 8, 10. The figure of 3000 annual trafficking victims for Israel is offered by The Parliamentary Investigation Committee on Trafficking in Women and is based on the number of prosecutions against perpetrators of human trafficking, so reflects only cases that have been investigated by the police.

p. 68 ranked Israel "very high": UNODC, 24.

p. 68 currently one of the top ten ... if they do not comply: Gijsbert Van Liemt, "Human Trafficking in Europe: An Economic Perspective" (Geneva: ILO, 2004), 5.

p. 68 an estimated 10,000 women: TIP (2006), 250; IOM, "Trafficking in Women and Children from the Republic of Armenia" (Geneva: IOM, 2001).

p. 68 Moldova is another ... and the Middle East: Irena Omelaniuk, "Trafficking in Human Beings" (New York: UN Expert Group

Meeting on International Migration and Development, 2005), 3; Eduard Mihailov et al., "Forced Labour Outcomes of Migration from Moldova" (Geneva: ILO, 2005).

p. 69 an estimated 35,000 women ... 400,000 Ukrainian women ... 11,000 trafficking victims: Kelly, 19.

p. 69 2100 Ukrainian victims: IOM, *Trafficking in Migrants Quarterly Bulletin* 23 (2001), 5.

p. 69 The UN notes that victims trafficked from African countries ... and Saudi Arabia: UNODC, 87.

p. 70 In South Africa, trafficked women ... mainly from West Africa: Jonathan Martens et al., "Seduction, Sale and Slavery: Trafficking in Women and Children for Sexual Exploitation in Southern Africa" (Geneva: IOM, 2003), 125, 6.

p. 70 The UN ranks Nigeria particularly high ... Morocco slightly less high: UNODC, 22.

p. 70 45,000 Nigerian women: Jorgen Carling, "Migration, Human Smuggling and Trafficking from Nigeria to Europe" (Geneva: IOM, 2006), 45.

p. 70 thirty-five percent ... twenty percent: UNODC, 86, 88.

p. 70 225,000 women and children: Annuska Derks, "Combating Trafficking in South-East Asia" (Geneva: IOM, 2000), 5.

p. 70 In Southern Asia, Sri Lankan women ...: TIP (2006), 186.

p. 70 up to 12,000 women and children: Jennifer Aengst, "Girl Trafficking in Nepal" (Denver: University of Denver Human Rights Advocacy Clinic, 2001), 2.

p. 70 200,000 trafficked Nepalese women and girls: ADB, "Combating Trafficking of Women and Children in South Asia: Nepal Report" (Manila: ADB, 2002), 21.

p. 70 internal sex trafficking victims: Ministry of Women, Children, and Social Welfare (WCSW), "National Plan of Action Against Trafficking in Children and Women for Sexual and Labour Exploitation" (Kathmandu: WCSW, 2001), 5.

p. 70 9368 trafficked women and children: Department of Women and Child Development, "Plan of Action to Combat Trafficking and Commercial Sexual Exploitation" (Delhi: Ministry of Human Resource Development, 1998). A report by the ADB points out that the Indian government's low estimate is due to low registration of trafficking crimes and the low priority that authorities give trafficking and related activities.

p. 71 one million women and children ... thirty percent: National Crime Records Bureau, "Crime In India" (Delhi: Ministry of Home Affairs, 2003).

p. 71 Cambodia is ranked high: UNODC, 89.

p. 71 Prostitution escalated in Cambodia ... sent to Thailand and Malaysia for forced prostitution: Eleanor Brown "The Ties that Bind; Migration and Trafficking of Women and Girls for Sexual Exploitation in Cambodia" (Geneva: IOM, 2007); Annuska Derks, "Trafficking of Vietnamese Women and Children to Cambodia" (Geneva: IOM, 1998).

p. 71 ranks Thailand even higher: UNODC, 103.

p. 71 "Thousands of women are also trafficked annually out of Thailand ...": Karen Tumlin, "Trafficking in Children in Asia: a Regional Overview" (Bangkok: Chulalongkorn University, 2000).

p. 72 only country in Eastern Asia that the UN ranks "very high": UNODC, 89.

p. 72 "phony marriages arranged ...": Tsutsumi and Honda, 34.

p. 72 Quotation from Nu: Bales and Trodd, 96.

p. 74 argues that all prostitution is forced: Mary Sullivan and Sheila Jeffreys, "Legalising Prostitution is Not the Answer: The Example of Victoria, Australia" (Victoria: CATW, 2000).

p. 75 "an adult woman is able to consent ...": The Human Rights Caucus, "Recommendations and Commentary on the Draft Protocol to Combat International Trafficking in Women and Children Supplementary to the Draft Convention on Transnational Organized Crime" (Geneva: UN, 1999), 5.

p. 75 "current federal law ... to end trafficking": Ann Jordan, "Testimony Before the House Subcommittee on Border, Maritime and Global Counterterrorism," Washington, DC, 20 March 2007.

p. 76 rates Germany "very high": UNODC, 34.

p. 76 expressed concern that there would be an increase: Jana Hennig et al., "Trafficking in Human Beings and the 2006 World Cup in Germany" (Geneva: IOM, 2007).

p. 77 policy has resulted in ...: Therese Hesketh et al., "The Effect of China's One-Child Family Policy after 25 Years," *New England Journal of Medicine* 353.11 (2005): 1171–6.

p. 77 thirty to ninety percent of marriages: Radhika Coomaraswamy, "Trafficking in Women and Forced Prostitution" (Geneva: UN, 2003).

p. 77 thousands of Sri Lankan women ... domestic servitude in private households: ASI, "Trafficking in Women, Forced Labour and Domestic Work in the Context of the Middle East and Gulf Region" (London: ASI, 2005).

p. 77 Quotation from Beatrice: Bales and Trodd, 161–2.

p. 78 The majority of domestic slaves ... precursor to commercial sex work: Kane, 15; Maggie Black, "A Handbook on Advocacy: Child Domestic Workers, Finding a Voice" (London: ASI, 2002), 5.

p. 78 fueled by the demand for ...: Bridget Anderson and Julia O'Connell Davidson, *Is Trafficking in Human Beings Demand Driven? A Multi-Country Pilot Study* (Geneva: IOM, 2003), 29–32.

p. 78 vulnerability is increased by ...: Joy M. Zarembka, "America's Dirty Work: Migrant Maids and Modern-Day Slavery," in Barbara Ehrenreich and Arlie Russell Hochschild (eds.), *Global Woman: Nannies, Maids, and Sex Workers in the New Economy* (New York: Metropolitan Books, 2002), 143–53.

p. 79 Quotation from Christina: Bales and Trodd, 154–6.

p. 80 US Justice Department announced the conviction ...: USJD Press Release, "Two Milwaukee Doctors Each Sentenced to Four Years in Prison for Forcing Woman to Work as Domestic Servant for 19 Years," 16 November 2006.

pp. 80–1 Quotations from Mende and Seba: Bales and Trodd, 227, 98.

p. 81 Women play a significant role as the enslavers ...: For one recent example of a woman enslaving another woman in domestic work, see Ruben Castaneda, "Woman Convicted of Enslaving Girl Flees," *Washington Post*, 3 March 2005: 2.

p. 81 in China, women are increasingly becoming involved ...: ILO, "Yunnan Province, China: Situation of Trafficking in Children and Women" (Geneva: ILO, 2002), viii.

p. 81 In India, many traffickers are older women ... fifty percent of people involved ...: Sankar Sen and P.M. Nair, "A Report on Trafficking in Women and Children in India" (Delhi: National Human Rights Commission/UN Development Fund for Women [UNIFEM]/ Institute of Social Sciences, 2004), 12, 354.

p. 81 two-thirds of traffickers in Cambodia: US Agency for International

Development (USAID), "International Justice Mission Anti-Trafficking Program in Cambodia Assessment" (Washington, DC: USAID, 2006), 7.

pp. 81–2 Quotations from Nu and Nuch: Bales and Trodd, 93, 85–6.

p. 82 more than a quarter of all traffickers: Europol, "Trafficking of Women and Children for Sexual Exploitation in the EU: The Involvement of Western Balkans Organised Crime" (Amsterdam: Europol, 2006), 19, 30.

p. 82 over half of all recruiters: IOM, "Victims of Trafficking in the Balkans" (Geneva: IOM, 2001), 53.

p. 82 In Moldova, more than half: Suzanna Banwell et al., "Trafficking in Women: Moldova and Ukraine" (Minneapolis: Minnesota Advocates for Human Rights, 2000), 24.

p. 82 Quotation from Milena: Bales and Trodd, 131, 133.

pp. 82–3 Quotations from Irina, Choti, and Shyamkali: Bales and Trodd, 213, 236, 238.

p. 83 willing to trade unwanted women and girls: A.K.M. Masud Ali, "Treading Along a Treacherous Trail: Research on Trafficking in Persons in South Asia," in Laczko and Gozdziak, 141–64 (147).

p. 84 Quotation from Anita: Bales and Trodd, 108.

p. 84 In Japan, few women ... other institutions: Jennifer Chan-Tiberghien, *Gender and Human Rights Politics in Japan: Global Norms and Domestic Networks* (Stanford: Stanford University Press, 2004).

p. 85 "interaction of poverty and gender-based ...": J.G. Silverman, M.R. Decker et al., "Experiences of Sex Trafficking Victims in Mumbai, India," *International Journal of Gynecology and Obstetrics* 97 (2007): 221–6 (221).

p. 85 All these factors ... difficulty supporting their families: FTS, "Recovering Childhoods: Combating Child Trafficking in Northern India" (Washington, DC: FTS, 2005).

p. 86 face community ostracism: Huma Ahmed-Ghosh, "Chattels of Society: Domestic Violence in India," *Violence Against Women* 10.1 (2004): 94–118; Rashmi Goel, "Sita's Trousseau: Restorative Justice, Domestic Violence, and South Asian Culture," *Violence Against Women* 11.5 (2005): 639–65.

p. 86 "fuelled by a supply of ... demand for women's and children's bodies": Alison Phinney, "Trafficking of Women and Children for

Sexual Exploitation in the Americas" (Washington, DC: Inter American Commission of Women, Women, Health and Development Programme, and World Health Organisation, 2001), 2.

p. 86 "Women's vulnerability to trafficking ...": Radhika Coomaraswamy, "Report to the World Conference against Racism, Racial Discrimination, Xenophobia and Related Intolerance" (Geneva: UN, 2001), 24.

p. 86 "liberalizing entry conditions enables ...": Gergana Danailova-Trainor and Patrick Belser, "Globalization and the Illicit Market for Human Trafficking: An Empirical Analysis of Supply and Demand" (Geneva: ILO, 2006), 8.

pp. 87–9 Quotations from Christine, Anita, Rita, and Alina: Bales and Trodd, 100–1, 109, 118, 126, 112.

p. 89 "many will stay in India ... seen as worthless": Peter Bashford, "A Sense of Direction: The Trafficking of Women and Children from Nepal" (Buckinghamshire: Asha-Nepal, 2006), 46.

p. 90 "the unequal status": Gillian Blackell, "The Protocols on Trafficking in Persons and Smuggling in Migrants," in Kathleen Macdonald and Monique Trépanier (eds.), *The Changing Face of International Criminal Law* (Vancouver: The International Centre for Criminal Law Reform and Criminal Justice Policy, 2002): 105–24 (122).

p. 90 "lack of rights afforded ...": Coomaraswamy (2001), 20.

Chapter 5

p. 92 43,000 individuals: ASI, "Slavery in Niger" (ASI: London: 2004), 1.

pp. 92–4 Quotations from Tamada, Selek'ha, and Oumoulkhér: Bales and Trodd, 159–60, 173, 174.

p. 95 Quotations from Salma: Bales and Trodd, 222, 225, 224.

p. 95 "sufficient to abolish the status ...": Abdel Weddoud Ould Cheikh, "L'evolution de l'esclavage dans la societe maure," in Edmond Bernus et al. (eds.), *Nomades et Commandants* (Paris: Karthala, 1993), 181–92 (192).

p. 96 between 5000 and 20,000 ... a tenth of the total: UNPFA, "Programming to Address Violence Against Women" (New York: UNPFA, 2006), 87.

p. 97 3500 slaves ... ninety percent of the 2000 *trokosis*: Ibid., 87–9.

p. 97 has been ineffective: Ibid., 88.

p. 97 17,000 girls: Bal Kumar KC, "Nepal Trafficking in Girls with Special Reference to Prostitution" (Geneva: ILO, 2001), 7.

p. 97 buy young girls from: Masud Ali, 147.

pp. 97–8 17,000 *devadasis* … 23,000 … 50,000: Maggie Black, "Women in Ritual Slavery: Devadasi, Jogini and Mathamma in Karnataka and Andhra Pradesh, Southern India" (London: ASI, 2007).

p. 98 Declared as "wives" of the gods … vulnerable to commercial sexual exploitation: Ravi Srivastava, "Bonded Labour in India: Its Incidence and Pattern" (Geneva: ILO, 2005); Sanlaap, "A Situational Analysis of Child Sex Tourism in India (Agra, Delhi, Jaipur)" (Bangkok: ECPAT International, 2003).

p. 99 Though officially outlawed … eviction, ostracization, and violence: Human Rights Watch (HRW) and the Center for Human Rights and Global Justice (CHRGJ) at New York University School of Law, "Hidden Apartheid: Caste Discrimination against India's 'Untouchables'" (New York: HRW and CHRGJ, 2007); S.K. Thorat, "Poverty, Caste and Child Labour in India: the Plight of Dalit and Adivasi Children," in Klaus Voll (ed.), *Against Child Labour: Indian and International Dimensions and Strategies* (Delhi: Third Millennium Transparency, 1999), 85–96.

p. 99 "behind the trafficking of women and children": FTS (2005), 23

p. 99 At least eighty percent of all … about age nine: ASI, "The Enslavement of Dalit and Indigenous Communities in India, Nepal and Pakistan Through Debt Bondage" (London: ASI, 2001); NGO Group for the Convention on the Rights of the Child, "The Impact of Discrimination on Working Children and on the Phenomenon of Child Labour" (Geneva: UN, 2002), 2; Sen and Nair, 100.

p. 99 has an ethnic component: Panudda Boonpala and June Kane, "Trafficking of Children: The Problem and Responses Worldwide" (Geneva: ILO, 2001), 22.

p. 99 In Romania, Bulgaria and Albania …: Omelaniuk, 5.

p. 100 most Nepalese slaves are from …: Kumar KC, 45.

p. 100 racial discrimination as "foreigners": UN Office of the High Commissioner for Human Rights, "Gender Dimensions of Racial Discrimination" (Geneva: UN, 2001), 13–14; Coomaraswamy (2001), 25.

p. 100 priced depending on their skin color: Carolina Johansson Wennerholm, "Crossing Borders and Building Bridges: the Baltic Region Networking Project," in Rachel Masika (ed.), *Gender, Trafficking and Slavery* (Oxford: Oxfam, 2002), 10–19 (13).

p. 100 "typically placed different groups ... and peasantry": Anderson and O'Connell, 21–22.

p. 101 higher in Muslim areas: Bashford, 43.

p. 101 In Thailand, slaveholders draw on ...: Jasmine Caye, "Preliminary Survey on Regional Child Trafficking for Prostitution in Thailand (Bangkok: UNICEF-EAPRO, 1995), 26.

p. 102 traffickers apply West African voodoo: Rijk Van Dijk, "Voodoo on the Doorstep Young Nigerian Prostitutes and Magic Policing in the Netherlands," *Africa* 71.4 (2001): 558–86; Francesco Prina, "Trade and Exploitation of Minors and Young Nigerian Women for Prostitution in Italy" (Geneva: UN, 2003).

pp. 102–3 Quotation from Joy: Bales and Trodd, 170–1.

p. 103 1045 camps ... one million people: The Laogai Research Foundation, *Laogai Handbook 2005–2006* (Washington, DC: Laogai Research Foundation, 2006), 6, 1.

p. 103 260,000: ILO (2005), 2.

p. 104 "[China] uses Laojiao ... refusing to work": Ramin Pejan, "Laogai: Reform Through Labor in China," *Human Rights Brief* 7.2 (2000): 22–3.

p. 104 Quotation from Sam: Bales and Trodd, 21.

p. 105 "continued to face arrest ...": DRL, "International Religious Freedom Report" (Washington, DC: USDS, 2007).

p. 105 from 10,000 to 100,000: Thomas Lum, "China and Falun Gong" (Washington, DC: Library of Congress, 2006), 4–5.

p. 105 half of the 250,000: Gretchen Birkle, "Testimony Before the House Committee on International Relations, Subcommittee on Africa, Global Human Rights and International Operations," Washington, DC, 21 July 2005.

Chapter 6

p. 107 eighty-five percent of conflict zones: Save the Children, "State of the World's Mothers" (Westport: Save the Children, 2003), 5.

p. 108 100,000 people: Bashford, 29, 32.

p. 108 ninety-five percent of displaced families: Save the Children, 11

p. 109 approximately four million: Martens et al., 21.

p. 109 sentences of twenty years: Coomaraswamy (2001), 34.

p. 109 "civil wars in the former Yugoslavia ... evidence of trafficking in this region": Europol, 8.

p. 109 slavery can flourish: Sue Nelson et al., "Literature Review and Analysis Related to Human Trafficking in Post-Conflict Situations" (Washington, DC: USAID, 2004), v.

p. 109 Another reason for the disproportionately high rate ... spurred a demand: Radhika Coomaraswamy, "Report of the Special Representative of the Secretary-General for Children and Armed Conflict" (Geneva: UN, 2007), 19; Vesna Nikolic-Ristanovic, *Social Change, Gender and Violence: Post-Communist and War-Affected Societies* (Boston: Kluwer, 2002), 130; UNPFA, "The Impact of Armed Conflict on Women and Girls" (Geneva: UN, 2001), 88; Omelaniuk, 3; Panagiota Tritaki, "Peacekeepers and Sex Trafficking: Supply and Demand in the Aftermath of the Kosovo Conflict" (Boston: Fletcher School of Law and Diplomacy, 2003).

p. 110 "displaced persons, widows and other ...": TIP, "Trafficking in Persons Report" (Washington, DC: USDS, 2003), 166.

p. 110 widespread trafficking, including ... Iraq for forced labor: Giuseppe Calandruccio, "A Review of Recent Research on Human Trafficking in the Middle East," in Laczko and Gozdziak, 267–99 (270); TIP (2006), 19; TIP (2007), 126.

p. 110 "has been a significant factor leading ...": Wendy Young, "Caught in the Crossfire: Displaced Colombians at Risk of Trafficking" (New York: Women's Commission for Refugee Women and Children, 2006), 11.

p. 111 50,000 Colombians trafficked ... fifteen percent ... 75,000 in Ecuador and 75,000 in Venezuela: Ibid., 1; Watchlist on Children and Armed Conflict (WCAC), "Colombia's War on Children" (New York: WCAC, 2004), 13.

p. 111 fifty percent are under eighteen years old: WCAC (2004), 3.

p. 111 35,000 internally displaced children: Young, 18.

p. 111 eighteen million children: UN, "Report of the Special Representative of the Secretary-General for Children and Armed Conflict" (Geneva: UN, 2007), 19.

p. 111 300,000 children: Hagemann, 26

p. 111 thirty current conflicts: ILO, "Wounded Childhood: The Use of Children in Armed Conflict in Central Africa" (Geneva: ILO, 2003), i; Sandrine Valentine, "Trafficking of Child Soldiers: Expanding the United Nations Convention on the Rights of the Child and its Optional Protocol on the Involvement of Children in Armed Conflict," *New England Journal of International and Comparative Law* 9.1 (2003): 109–34 (119, 120).

p. 112 These child soldiers are usually from ... then Europe: Valentine, 117, 127, 110; Coalition to Stop the Use of Child Soldiers (CSC), "Child Soldier Use 2003: A Briefing for the 4th UN Security Council Open Debate on Children and Armed Conflict (London: CSC, 2003), 2; Susan McKay and Dyan Mazurana, "Girls in Militaries, Paramilitaries, and Armed Opposition Groups" (Ottawa: Department of Foreign Affairs and International Trade, 2001), 5.

p. 112 40,000 children ... 30,000: CSC, "Child Soldiers Global Report" (London: CSC, 2004), 13, 15.

p. 112 11,000 and 14,000 ... several thousand under the age of fifteen ... up to one-third of some units: WCAC (2004), 26, 27, 14.

p. 113 Half of all recruits to the armed opposition: Young, 12, 18; Valentine, 123.

p. 113 Armed political groups also abduct ... members are now children: CSC (2004), 17, 18, 190, 201; DRL, "Country Reports on Human Rights Practices: Philippines" (Washington, DC: USDS, 2007), 1.

p. 113 over forty percent girls ... Up to sixty percent of dead fighters: Jo Becker and Tejshree Thapa, "Living in Fear: Child Soldiers and the Tamil Tigers in Sri Lanka" (New York: HRW, 2004), 6.

p. 114 3500 new cases ... 1200 children ... one in nineteen: Ibid., 3, 2, 16.

p. 114 LTTE had still not ceased: UN (2007), 9.

p. 114 There are many more child soldiers in Africa ... into Liberian society: CSC (2004), 31 24, 76; ILO (2003), 4, 17.

p. 115 In the DRC ... within the government's army and the rebel groups: CSC (2004), 51, 52; CSC, "International Forum on Armed Groups and the Involvement of Children in Armed Conflict" (London: CSC, 2007), 14.

p. 115 the LRA has abducted 25,000 children ... due to injury or age: UN (2007), 19; Survey of War Affected Youth (SWAY), "Research and

Programs for Youth in Armed Conflict in Uganda: The Abduction and Return Experiences of Youth" (Berkeley: SWAY, 2006), 6; CSC (2003), 45; CSC (2004), 21; WCAC, "Sudan's Children at a Crossroads: An Urgent Need for Protection" (New York: WCAC, 2007), 10.

p. 116 government itself recruits: CSC (2004), 17.

p. 117 13,500 child soldiers ... estimated 17,000 children: Bureau of African Affairs, "Slavery, Abduction and Forced Servitude in Sudan" (Washington, DC: USDS, 2002), 7, 10, 26, 27; CSC (2004), 31; WCAC (2007), 58.

p. 117 In January 2005, a peace agreement ... running into the thousands: UN (2007), 22; WCAC (2007), 2, 6, 42.

p. 117 12,000 abductions from southern Sudan ... estimates of abductees ranging from 10,000 to 200,000: ASI, "Report to the United Nations Commission on Human Rights: Forced Labour and Slavery of Women and Children in Sudan" (London: ASI, 2002); ASI, "Report to the United Nations Commission on Human Rights: Abductions and Forced Labour in Sudan" (London: ASI, 2004); Bureau of African Affairs, 42; WCAC (2007), 58, 56.

p. 118 slave labor has been widespread in Burma ...: DRL, "Country Reports on Human Rights Practices: Burma" (Washington, DC: USDS, 2006); TIP (2007), 34, 71.

p. 119 Unocal settled out of court: John Crood, "Tentative Settlement of ATCA Human Rights Suits against Unocal," *The American Journal of International Law* 99.2 (2005): 497–498.

p. 119 70,000 children ... 45 percent of new recruits ... tens of thousands: CSC (2003), 2, 27; CSC (2004), 18.

p. 119 Burma refused to cease kidnapping children ...: TIP (2006), 28.

p. 119 destroyed Burma's mountain forests: Center for International Environmental Law (CIEL), "Environmental Justice and Sustainable Development" (Washington, DC: CIEL, 2002), 8.

p. 120 South American forests are cut and burned: You can see a Brazilian charcoal camp in Moto Grosso do Sul, using Google Earth and its satellite and aerial photographs. The GPS coordinates are: 19°52'14.22" South 53°03'30.84" West. The beehive shaped domes of the low ovens used to burn the forests into charcoal for use in the steel industry are lined up on each side of a dirt road. Smoke is rising from the ovens, and the ground is blackened near the road where charcoal has been spilt. To the east of the camp you can see where the forest has been clear cut to feed the ovens.

p. 121 displace between 250,000 and one million people: Subodh Wagle, "The Long March for Livelihoods: Struggle Against the Narmada Dam in India," in John Byrne et al. (eds.), *Environmental Justice: Discourses in International Political Economy Energy and Environmental Policy* (New Brunswick: Transaction, 2002), 71–96 (72).

pp. 121–2 Elsewhere in India ... from that region increased: Javita Narang, "Human Trafficking and HIV: Exploring Vulnerabilities and Responses in South Asia" (Columbo: UNDP, 2007), 50; Yasmeen Mohiuddin, "Human Trafficking: Slavery in the Twenty-First Century" (South Africa: Fotim International Conference, 2006), 6.

Chapter 7

p. 124 "has a devastating impact ...": TIP (2007), 5.

p. 124 "the health, safety ...": Ibid.

pp. 125–6 Study that followed nearly 150 London-based female prostitutes: Helen Ward and Sophie E. Day, "What Happens to Women Who Sell Sex? Report of a Unique Occupational Cohort," *Sexually Transmitted Infections* 82.5 (2006): 413–17.

p. 126 Study on violence and rape in prostitution: Melissa Farley et al., "Prostitution and Trafficking in Nine Countries: An Update on Violence and Posttraumatic Stress Disorder," *Journal of Trauma Practice* 2.3 (2003): 33–74.

p. 126 Study assessing brothel-based sex workers in West Bengal: Kamalesh Sarkar et al., "Young Age is a Risk Factor for HIV Among Female Sex Workers: An Experience from India," *Journal of Infection* 53.4 (2006): 255–9.

p. 127 first cases of AIDS were reported: Centers for Disease Control and Prevention, "Pneumocystis Pneumonia—Los Angeles," *Morbidity and Mortality Weekly Report* 30.21 (1981): 250–2.

p. 127 HIV/AIDS statistics: UN Programme on HIV/AIDS (UNAIDS) and World Health Organization (WHO), "Aids Epidemic Update" (Geneva: UNAIDS and WHO, 2007), 21–36.

p. 127 fourteen million orphans: Beyrer, 16–17.

p. 128 Study of 175 females: J.G. Silverman et al., "HIV Prevalence and Predictors Among Rescued Sex-Trafficked Women and Girls in Mumbai, India," *Journal of Acquired Immune Deficiency Syndrome* 43.5 (2006): 588–93. The percentage of females who tested positive for HIV (22.9 percent) may underestimate the actual prevalence of HIV infection in this population due to a short time interval between their rescue and their HIV testing, which may not allow measurable levels of HIV antibody to develop in the blood.

p. 128 Study of nearly 300 repatriated Nepalese girls and women: J.G. Silverman et al., "HIV Prevalence and Predictors of Infection in Sex-Trafficked Nepalese Girls and Women," *Journal of the American Medical Association* 298.5 (2007): 536–42. The percentage of females who tested positive for HIV (~40 percent) more reliably estimates the actual prevalence of HIV infection in this population as the time interval between their rescue and their HIV testing was sufficiently long to allow measurable levels of HIV antibody to develop in the blood.

p. 129 Quotation from Dina: Bales and Trodd, 106.

p. 129 prefer not to wear condoms ...: Karen Leiter et al., "No Status: Migration, Trafficking and Exploitation of Women in Thailand—Health and HIV/AIDS Risks for Burmese and Hill Tribe Women and Girls" (Boston: Physicians for Human Rights, 2004), 38.

p. 129 prepubescent and pubertal girls are in high demand ...: Aengst, 8.

p. 130 forced to douche ...: Michael Rekart, "Sex-Work Harm Reduction," *Lancet* 366.9503 (2005): 2123–34 (2124).

p. 130 four-fold increased risk: Brian Willis and Barry Levy, "Child Prostitution: Global Health Burden, Research Needs, and Interventions," *Lancet* 359.9315 (2002): 1417–22.

p. 130 Quotations from Maria and Nu: Bales and Trodd, 185, 95.

p. 131 ninety percent ... will become pregnant: Willis and Levy, 1419.

p. 131 "preventable pandemic": David A. Grimes et al., "Unsafe Abortion: the Preventable Pandemic," *Lancet* 368.9550 (2006): 1908–19.

pp. 131–2 Quotations from Nu and Jill: Bales and Trodd, 95, 178, 177, 94.

p. 133 "promotion of health ... camel jockeys": Bebe Loff and Jyoti Sanghera, "Distortions and Difficulties in Data for Trafficking," *Lancet* 363.9408 (2004): 566.

p. 133 up to forty-seven percent: FTS and HRC, 35, 36.

p. 133 1.5 million people: Christopher Dye et al., "Global Tuberculosis Control: Surveillance, Planning, Financing" (Geneva: WHO, 2007).

p. 133 In April 2008 ...: Ian MacKinnon, "54 Burmese Migrants Suffocate in Packed Lorry," *Guardian*, 11 April 2008: 16.

p. 135 Quotations from Ashok and Ying: Bales and Trodd, 78, 24.

p. 136 one out of every two childhood deaths: WHO, "Nutrition: Challenges" (Geneva: WHO, 2005), 1.

p. 137 Quotations from Rambho, Ravi, and Ashok: Bales and Trodd, 72, 75–6, 78.

p. 138 nearly ninety percent of women trafficked: Raymond and Hughes, 81.

p. 138 over forty percent of prostituted adolescent girls: Willis and Levy, 1419.

pp. 138–9 Quotations from Jill, Nu and Inez: Bales and Trodd, 179–80, 94, 183, 179.

p. 139 psychoactive drugs: for examples see narratives by Ying and Maria in Bales and Trodd, 26, 51.

p. 139 Complex PTSD has the following symptoms: 1. Alterations in the ability to regulate or control emotions, expressed as sadness, suicidal thoughts, or explosive anger. 2. Changes in consciousness, including forgetting traumatic events, reliving traumatic events, or having periods when the victim feels detached from his or her own body and mental processes. Confusion about the history of traumatic events also occurs; this, plus the forgetting of events, makes it challenging for the victim of human trafficking to effectively participate in the legal process. 3. Altered perception of the perpetrator, such as attributing total power to the perpetrator or becoming preoccupied with the victim–perpetrator relationship. This altered perception may also prevent the victim from effectively participating in the legal process. 4. Changes in self-perception, including a sense of helplessness, shame, guilt, and stigma. Those who have suffered prolonged captivity and abuse may develop a sense that they are completely different from other human beings. 5. Changes in relations with others, including distrust and social isolation. 6. A shattering of the victim's system of meaning, a loss of faith, or a sense of hopelessness. Adapted from Julia M. Whealin and Laurie Slone, "Complex PTSD" (Washington, DC: US Department of Veterans Affairs, 2007).

p. 139 nearly seventy percent of prostituted women ...: Farley et al., 34.

p. 140 "fitted together like a mosaic": Helga Konrad, "Combating Trafficking in Human Beings – Learning from the European Experience" (Geneva: ILO, 2003), 7.

p. 141 "[forensic] examination must be carefully planned …": Djordie Alempijevic et al., "Forensic Medical Examination of Victims of Trafficking in Human Beings," *Torture* 17.2 (2007): 117–21 (118–19).

p. 142 "such analysis is helpful …": Ibid., 121.

p. 143 "Rescue and Restore Campaign": see www.acf.hhs.gov/trafficking. Guidelines for interviews are available in Cathy Zimmerman and Charlotte Watts, "WHO Ethical and Safety Recommendations for Interviewing Trafficked Women" (Geneva: WHO, 2003).

p. 143 PREVENT mnemonic: Willis and Levy, 1421.

Chapter 8

p. 146 "our struggle is easier than …": John R. Miller, "Remarks at the Underground Railroad Freedom Center Dedication, Cincinnati, Ohio," 23 August 2004, National Archives and Records Administration (NARA).

p. 149 5000 people … 7000: Bhavna Sharma, "Contemporary Forms of Slavery in Brazil" (London: ASI, 2006), 3.

p. 156 We can buy survivor-made goods …: see www.madebysurvivors.com.

p. 158 third good example of this method: Jean-Paul Sajhau, "Business Ethics in the Textile, Clothing and Footwear Industries: Codes of Conduct" (Geneva: ILO, 2000), sec. 5.

p. 158 5.5 million carpets … 3000 children: Rugmark USA, "Annual Report" (New York: Rugmark, 2006), 4.

p. 161 Some possible questions you could ask: adapted from the US Department of Health and Human Services "Rescue and Restore" campaign. If you hear about or uncover what you think could be a trafficking situation, the best course is to call a trained professional. In the US, the Trafficking Information and Referral Toll-Free Hotline is open twenty-four hours, on 1–888–373–7888. You can also report trafficking crimes at the Trafficking in Persons and Worker Exploitation Task Force Complaint Line, 1–888–428–7581. In the UK, call Crimestoppers at 0800–555–111.

p. 164 organizations that liberate slaves: Anti-slavery organizations are listed in appendix C of this book.

p. 164 $130 … $400: These costs are from the current budgets of FTS and its grass-roots partners.

p. 166 "When one takes on a challenge … this modern scourge": Miller, "Speech at Swearing-in as Senior Advisor to the Secretary of State and Director of the Office to Monitor and Combat Trafficking in Persons," 4 March 2003.

p. 166 "The struggle will be a long one … new abolitionist movement": Miller (2004).

p. 166 "the two-hundredth anniversary … human beings from slavery": Kofi Annan, "Information Release 54/06: The International Day for the Abolition of Slavery, 2 December 2006" (Geneva: UN), 1.

pp. 166–7 "We need hundreds of Wilberforces …": Miller, "Call It Slavery," *The Wilson Quarterly*, Summer 2008: 52–6 (56).

Further reading

Anderson, Bridget. *Doing the Dirty Work? The Global Politics of Domestic Labour*. London: Zed, 2000.

Anker, Christien Van Den. *The Political Economy of New Slavery*. New York: Palgrave Macmillan, 2004.

Bales, Kevin. *Disposable People: New Slavery in the Global Economy*. Berkeley: University of California Press, 1999.

Bales, Kevin. *Ending Slavery: How We Free Today's Slaves*. Berkeley: University of California Press, 2007.

Bales, Kevin and Zoe Trodd, eds. *To Plead Our Own Cause: Personal Stories by Today's Slaves*. Ithaca: Cornell University Press, 2008.

Blackmon, Douglas A. *Slavery by Another Name: The Re-Enslavement of Black Americans from the Civil War to World War II*. New York: Doubleday, 2008.

Bok, Francis and Edward Tivnan. *Escape from Slavery: the True Story of My Ten Years in Captivity and My Journey to Freedom in America*. New York: St. Martin's Press, 2003.

Cadet, Jean-Robert. *Restavec: From Haitian Slave Child to Middle-Class American, An Autobiography*. Austin: University of Texas Press, 1998.

Eltis, David, ed. *Coerced and Free Migration: Global Perspectives*. Stanford: Stanford University Press, 2002.

Gardner, Martha. *The Qualities of a Citizen: Women, Immigration, and Citizenship, 1870–1965*. Princeton: Princeton University Press, 2005.

Guinn, David E. and Elissa Steglich, eds. *In Modern Bondage: Sex Trafficking in the Americas*. New York: Transnational Publishers, 2003.

Hochschild, Adam. *King Leopold's Ghost*. New York: Houghton Mifflin, 1998.

Jok, Jok Madut. *War and Slavery in Sudan*. Philadelphia: University of Pennsylvania Press, 2001.

Kara, Siddharth. *Sex Trafficking: Inside the Business of Modern Slavery*. New York: Columbia University Press, 2009.

Klein, Martin, ed. *Breaking the Chains: Slavery, Bondage, and Emancipation in Modern Africa and Asia*. Madison: University of Wisconsin Press, 1993.

Lebreton, Binka. *Trapped: Modern-Day Slavery in the Brazilian Amazon*. Bloomfield: Kumarian Press, 2003.

Miers, Suzanne. *Slavery in the Twentieth Century: The Evolution of a Global Problem*. Walnut Creek: Alta Mira Press, 2003.

Nazer, Mende and Damien Lewis. *Slave: My True Story*. New York: Public Affairs, 2003.

Ruf, Urs Peter. *Ending Slavery: Hierarchy, Dependency and Gender in Central Mauritania*. Bielefeld: Transcript Verlag, 1999.

Sawyer, Roger. *Slavery in the Twentieth Century*. London: Routledge & Kegan Paul, 1986.

Skinner, E. Benjamin. *A Crime So Monstrous: Face-to-Face with Modern-Day Slavery*. New York: Simon and Schuster, 2008.

Glossary

Chattel slavery One person assumes complete ownership over another, and the slave is considered property of the slaveholder.

Child soldier Any person under the age of eighteen who is a member of or attached to government armed forces or any other regular or irregular armed force or armed political group.

Cocoa Protocol An agreement to eliminate slavery and the worst forms of child labor from cocoa production in West Africa by 2005, signed by the global chocolate industry, several NGOs, organized labor, the International Labour Organisation (ILO), two US Senators, and an Ivory Coast ambassador.

Convention or covenant Agreements in international law between independent countries.

Debt bondage slavery or bonded labor A situation where a person is forced to give him or herself and his or her family as collateral against a debt and thus comes under the complete control of the money-lender. Since the work he or she does is already the property of the money-lender, it becomes impossible to pay off the debt and it is passed down, enslaving following generations.

Forced labor All work or service which is exacted from a person under the menace of penalty and which is undertaken involuntarily.

Human trafficking The transport of a person from one place to another, often a foreign country, through deception or force in order to enslave them.

Internally displaced persons People who have been forced to flee their homes for reasons such as armed conflict, human rights abuses, or natural disasters, and who have sought safety elsewhere in the same country.

Migrant laborer   A person who works in a country where he or she is not a citizen.

Nongovernmental Organization (NGO)   Independent organizations that are not part of any state or interstate agency. They include charities, nonprofit organizations, voluntary groups, professional associations, trades unions, and human rights bodies.

Restavecs   Children in Haiti who are given or sold by their parents into domestic work for another family.

Serfdom   The condition where agricultural workers cannot leave the place where they live and work, and are traditionally obliged to work for others for little or no reward.

Servile marriage   When a girl or woman has no right to refuse a marriage.

Sex trafficking   The recruitment, harboring, transportation, provision, or obtaining of a person for the purpose of a commercial sex act.

Slavery   A social and economic relationship in which a person is controlled through violence or its threat, paid nothing beyond subsistence, and is economically exploited.

Slave trade   All acts involved in the capture, acquisition, or disposal of a person with intent to reduce him or her to slavery.

Smuggling of migrants   The procurement, in order to obtain a financial or other material benefit, of the illegal entry of a person into a country of which the person is not a national or a permanent resident.

Untouchables or outcasts   Those in Hindu society, primarily in India, who do not belong to one of the four major Hindu castes. Untouchables, now normally referred to as "Dalits," suffer regular discrimination and their exclusion from education and jobs means that they are especially vulnerable to enslavement.

Worst forms of child labor ILO term referring to child labor that involves slavery, trafficking, forced labor, child soldiers, commercial sexual exploitation of children, children used for illegal activities, or other work that harms children's health and morals.

Appendix A: timeline

c. 2575 BC	Egyptians send slave-raiding expeditions down the Nile River.
c. 550 BC	In Athens, the Greeks use around 30,000 slaves in the city-state's silver mines.
c. 120	The Roman military captures thousands of slaves during military campaigns.
c. 1000	In rural England, poor agricultural workers and their families are held in debt bondage to wealthy landowners.
c. 1250	Between 5000 and 25,000 slaves are taken from West Africa to the Mediterranean in the trans-Saharan slave trade, where they go on to be sold in Europe and the Middle East.
c. 1380	After the Black Plague, the slave trade in Europe starts to address the labor shortage. Slaves are brought from Europe, the Middle East, and North Africa.
c. 1444	The first slaves are brought to Europe from West Africa in the beginning of the Atlantic slave trade.
1619	Slavery in the American colonies begins with the delivery of twenty Africans to the English settlement at Jamestown, Virginia. Other countries involved in the European slave trade are Holland (from 1625), France (from 1642), Sweden (from 1647), and Denmark (from 1697).
1803	Denmark bans the African slave trade, becoming the first country in Europe to do so. Danish citizens

	are forbidden from trading in slaves and the importation of slaves into Danish dominions is ended.
1807	The British Parliament bans British ships from transporting slaves and British colonies from importing slaves.
1808	The United States ends the importation of Africans as slaves. By this time there are around one million slaves in the country.
1814	The Netherlands officially ends Dutch participation in the African slave trade.
1820	Spain ends the slave trade in areas south of the Equator, but continues slavery in Cuba until 1888.
1825	Slavery is abolished in Argentina, Bolivia, Chile, and Peru.
1833	Slavery is abolished throughout the British Empire. About $100 million is paid to slave owners as compensation for their losses.
1840	The World Anti-Slavery Convention is held in London.
1848	France abolishes slavery in the country and its colonies.
1850	Brazil ends its involvement in the slave trade.
1863	The "Emancipation Proclamation," delivered by President Abraham Lincoln during the American Civil War, frees all slaves in the Confederate states.
1863	The Netherlands abolishes slavery in all its colonies.
1888	Brazil emancipates 725,000 slaves in the country, ending slavery in South America.
1910	In Paris, the "International Convention for the Suppression of the White Slave Trade" is signed. The signatories promise to punish anyone who enlists an underage woman into prostitution, even if she consents.
1915	The colony of Malaya abolishes slavery.
1923	Hong Kong bans the sale of young girls as domestic slaves.

1926	The "Slavery Convention" is passed by the League of Nations, obligating member countries to work to end all forms of slavery.
1926	Burma abolishes slavery.
1927	Sierra Leone abolishes slavery.
1936	The King of Saudi Arabia ends the importation of new slaves into the country and regulates the treatment of slaves already in the country, instead of abolishing slavery.
1938–1945	Thousands of Korean and Chinese women are forced to become slaves in Japanese military "comfort stations," or brothels.
1939–1945	The Nazi government in Germany uses slaves during World War II in farming and industry.
1948	The Universal Declaration of Human Rights is passed by the United Nations (UN). It includes the assertion "no one shall be held in slavery or servitude; slavery and the slave trade shall be prohibited in all their forms."
1954	China begins allowing prisoners to be used as laborers in its *laogai* camps.
1962	Saudi Arabia and Yemen abolish slavery.
1974	Freed slaves in Mauritania begin a group called El Hor, meaning "freedom," to oppose slavery.
1975	The UN establishes the Working Group on Contemporary Forms of Slavery, which gathers information and makes recommendations about slavery around the world.
1976	Bonded labor is abolished in India.
1989	The UN adopts the "Convention on the Rights of the Child."
1990	The UN adopts the "Convention on the Protection of the Rights of All Migrant Workers and Members of Their Families."
1991	The UN establishes the Voluntary Trust Fund on Contemporary Forms of Slavery. Its purpose is to

assist NGOs dealing with contemporary forms of slavery and to provide humanitarian, legal, and financial aid to victims.

1992	Pakistan ends indentured servitude and the peshgi (bonded money) system.
1995	The Rugmark Foundation is launched.
1997	The UN creates a commission to investigate allegations of the enslavement of people by the Burmese government.
1997	The US bans the importation of goods made by child bonded laborers.
1999	The UN announces December 2 as the "International Day for the Abolition of slavery." The International Labour Organisation (ILO) establishes international standards for protecting children from forced labor, prostitution, and other harmful work in the "Convention Against the Worst Forms of Child Labor."
2000	Nepal abolishes all forms of debt bondage. The UN adopts the "Protocol to Prevent, Suppress, and Punish Trafficking in Persons, Especially Women and Children." The US Congress passes the "Trafficking Victims Protection Act" (TVPA), which establishes the crime of human trafficking and sets out benefits and protections for victims.
2001	The US State Department's Office to Monitor and Combat Trafficking in Persons releases its first annual "Trafficking in Persons Report." The annual report, required by Congress under the TVPA, provides an overview of anti-trafficking measures worldwide.
2002	NGOs, chocolate companies, and local governments form the International Cocoa Initiative to enforce the protocol and monitor production. The "Optional Protocol on the Sale of Children, Child Prostitution and Child Pornography," and the

"Optional Protocol on the Involvement of Children in Armed Conflict," both supplements to the UN's "Convention on the Rights of the Child," enter into force.

2003   The US enacts economic sanctions against Burma for the government's use of forced labor.

2004   The US proposes 27 February as "National Anti-Slavery Day."

2005   The ILO publishes the first global report on forced labor.

2006   Actress Julia Ormond is appointed first UN Goodwill Ambassador for the Abolition of Slavery and Human Trafficking. Manpower Inc., an international employment services industry, asks 1000 of the world's largest companies to help end human trafficking.

2007   The US State Department announces that in the fiscal year 2006, it gave $74 million to 154 international anti-human trafficking projects in seventy countries and $28.5 million to seventy domestic anti-human trafficking projects. The UK observes an "Anti-Slavery Day" on 25 March.

2008   The US observes 11 January as the first annual "National Human Trafficking Awareness Day."

Appendix B: anti-slavery legislation

League of Nations, "Slavery Convention" (1926)

Article 2. The High Contracting Parties undertake:

(a) To prevent and suppress the slave trade;
(b) To bring about, progressively and as soon as possible, the complete abolition of slavery in all its forms.

Article 3. The High Contracting Parties undertake to adopt all appropriate measures with a view to preventing and suppressing the embarkation, disembarkation and transport of slaves in their territorial waters and upon all vessels flying their respective flags.

Article 5. The High Contracting Parties undertake to take all necessary measures to prevent compulsory or forced labour from developing into conditions analogous to slavery.

ILO, "Convention no. 29, concerning forced labour" (1930)

Article 1. Each Member of the International Labour Organisation which ratifies this Convention undertakes to suppress the use of forced or compulsory labour in all its forms within the shortest possible period.

Article 4. The competent authority shall not impose or permit the imposition of forced or compulsory labour for the benefit of private individuals, companies or associations.

UN, "Supplementary convention on the abolition of slavery, the slave trade, and institutions and practices similar to slavery" (1956)

Article 1. Each of the States Parties to this Convention shall ... bring about progressively and as soon as possible the complete abolition or abandonment of the following institutions and practices:

(a) Debt bondage
(b) Serfdom
(c) Any institution or practice whereby:

    (i) A woman, without the right to refuse, is promised or given in marriage on payment of a consideration in money or in kind to her parents, guardian, family or any other person or group; or

    (ii) The husband of a woman, his family, or his clan, has the right to transfer her to another person for value received or otherwise; or

    (iii) A woman on the death of her husband is liable to be inherited by another person;

(d) Any institution or practice whereby a child or young person under the age of 18 years, is delivered by either or both of his natural parents or by his guardian to another person, whether for reward or not, with a view to the exploitation of the child or young person or of his labour.

Article 6. The act of enslaving another person or of inducing another person to give himself or a person dependent upon him into slavery, or of attempting these acts, or being accessory thereto ... shall be a criminal offence.

ILO, "Convention no. 105, concerning the abolition of forced labour" (1957)

Article 1. Each Member of the International Labour Organisation which ratifies this Convention undertakes to suppress and not to make use of any form of forced or compulsory labour:

(a) As a means of political coercion or education or as a punishment for holding or expressing political views or views ideologically opposed to the established political, social, or economic system;
(b) As a method of mobilising and using labour for purposes of economic development;
(c) As a means of labour discipline;
(d) As a punishment for having participated in strikes;
(e) As a means of racial, social, national or religious discrimination.

Article 2. Each Member undertakes to take effective measures to secure the immediate and complete abolition of forced or compulsory labour as specified in article 1 of this Convention.

ILO, "Convention no. 182, concerning the worst forms of child labour" (1999)

Article 1. Each Member which ratifies this Convention shall take immediate and effective measures to secure the prohibition and elimination of the worst forms of child labour as a matter of urgency.

Article 3. The term "the worst forms of child labour" comprises:

(a) all forms of slavery or practices similar to slavery, such as the sale and trafficking of children, debt bondage and serfdom and forced or compulsory labour, including forced or compulsory recruitment of children for use in armed conflict;
(b) the use, procuring or offering of a child for prostitution, for the production of pornography or for pornographic performances;
(c) the use, procuring or offering of a child for illicit activities, in particular for the production and trafficking of drugs as defined in the relevant international treaties;
(d) work which, by its nature or the circumstances in which it is carried out, is likely to harm the health, safety or morals of children.

Article 6. Each Member shall design and implement programmes of action to eliminate as a priority the worst forms of child labour.

Article 7. Each Member shall … take effective and time-bound measures to:

(a) prevent the engagement of children in the worst forms of child labour;

(b) provide the necessary and appropriate direct assistance for the removal of children from the worst forms of child labour and for their rehabilitation and social integration;

(c) ensure access to free basic education, and, wherever possible and appropriate, vocational training, for all children removed from the worst forms of child labour;

(d) identify and reach out to children at special risk; and

(e) take account of the special situation of girls.

Article 8. Members shall take appropriate steps to assist one another in giving effect to the provisions of this Convention through enhanced international cooperation and/or assistance including support for social and economic development, poverty eradication programmes and universal education.

UN, "Protocol to prevent, suppress and punish trafficking in persons, especially women and children, supplementing the UN convention against transnational organised crime" (2000)

Article 2. The purposes of this Protocol are:

(a) To prevent and combat trafficking in persons, paying particular attention to women and children;

(b) To protect and assist the victims of such trafficking, with full respect for their human rights; and

(c) To promote cooperation among States Parties in order to meet those objectives.

Article 3. For the purposes of this Protocol:

(a) "Trafficking in persons" shall mean the recruitment, transportation, transfer, harbouring or receipt of persons, by means of the threat or use of force or other forms of coercion, of abduction, of fraud, of deception, of the abuse of power or of a position of vulnerability or of the giving or receiving of payments or benefits to achieve the consent of a person having control over another person, for the purpose of exploitation. Exploitation shall include, at a minimum, the exploitation of the prostitution of others or other forms of sexual exploitation, forced labour or services, slavery or practices similar to slavery, servitude or the removal of organs;

(b) The consent of a victim of trafficking in persons to the intended exploitation set forth in subparagraph (a) of this article shall be irrelevant where any of the means set forth in subparagraph (a) have been used;

(c) The recruitment, transportation, transfer, harbouring or receipt of a child for the purpose of exploitation shall be considered "trafficking in persons" even if this does not involve any of the means set forth in subparagraph (a) of this article;

(d) "Child" shall mean any person under eighteen years of age.

Article 4. This Protocol shall apply, except as otherwise stated herein, to the prevention, investigation and prosecution of the offences established in accordance with article 5 of this Protocol, where those offences are transnational in nature and involve an organized criminal group, as well as to the protection of victims of such offences.

Article 5

1. Each State Party shall adopt such legislative and other measures as may be necessary to establish as criminal offences the conduct set forth in article 3 of this Protocol, when committed intentionally.

Article 6

1. In appropriate cases and to the extent possible under its domestic law, each State Party shall protect the privacy and identity of

victims of trafficking in persons, including, inter alia, by making legal proceedings relating to such trafficking confidential.

2. Each State Party shall ensure that its domestic legal or administrative system contains measures that provide to victims of trafficking in persons, in appropriate cases:

    (a) Information on relevant court and administrative proceedings;
    (b) Assistance to enable their views and concerns to be presented and considered at appropriate stages of criminal proceedings against offenders, in a manner not prejudicial to the rights of the defence.

3. Each State Party shall consider implementing measures to provide for the physical, psychological and social recovery of victims of trafficking in persons, including, in appropriate cases, in cooperation with non-governmental organizations, other relevant organizations and other elements of civil society, and, in particular, the provision of:

    (a) Appropriate housing;
    (b) Counselling and information, in particular as regards their legal rights, in a language that the victims of trafficking in persons can understand;
    (c) Medical, psychological and material assistance; and
    (d) Employment, educational and training opportunities.

Article 9

1. States Parties shall establish comprehensive policies, programmes and other measures:

    (a) To prevent and combat trafficking in persons; and
    (b) To protect victims of trafficking in persons, especially women and children, from revictimization.

2. States Parties shall endeavour to undertake measures such as research, information and mass media campaigns and social and economic initiatives to prevent and combat trafficking in persons.

3. Policies, programmes and other measures established in accordance with this article shall, as appropriate, include cooperation with non-governmental organizations, other relevant organizations and other elements of civil society.
4. States Parties shall take or strengthen measures, including through bilateral or multilateral cooperation, to alleviate the factors that make persons, especially women and children, vulnerable to trafficking, such as poverty, underdevelopment and lack of equal opportunity.
5. States Parties shall adopt or strengthen legislative or other measures, such as educational, social or cultural measures, including through bilateral and multilateral cooperation, to discourage the demand that fosters all forms of exploitation of persons, especially women and children, that leads to trafficking.

US Congress, "victims of trafficking and violence protection act" (2000)
SEC. 102. Purposes and findings.

Congress finds that:

(1) As the 21st century begins, the degrading institution of slavery continues throughout the world. Trafficking in persons is a modern form of slavery […]
(2) Many of these persons are trafficked into the international sex trade, often by force, fraud, or coercion. The sex industry has rapidly expanded over the past several decades. It involves sexual exploitation of persons, predominantly women and girls, involving activities related to prostitution, pornography, sex tourism, and other commercial sexual services. The low status of women in many parts of the world has contributed to a burgeoning of the trafficking industry.
(3) Trafficking in persons is not limited to the sex industry. This growing transnational crime also includes forced labor and

involves significant violations of labor, public health, and human rights standards worldwide.

(4) Traffickers primarily target women and girls, who are disproportionately affected by poverty, the lack of access to education, chronic unemployment, discrimination, and the lack of economic opportunities in countries of origin. Traffickers lure women and girls into their networks through false promises of decent working conditions at relatively good pay as nannies, maids, dancers, factory workers, restaurant workers, sales clerks, or models. Traffickers also buy children from poor families and sell them into prostitution or into various types of forced or bonded labor.

(5) Traffickers often transport victims from their home communities to unfamiliar destinations, including foreign countries away from family and friends, religious institutions, and other sources of protection and support, leaving the victims defenseless and vulnerable.

(6) Victims are often forced through physical violence to engage in sex acts or perform slavery-like labor. Such force includes rape and other forms of sexual abuse, torture, starvation, imprisonment, threats, psychological abuse, and coercion.

(7) Traffickers often make representations to their victims that physical harm may occur to them or others should the victim escape or attempt to escape. Such representations can have the same coercive effects on victims as direct threats to inflict such harm.

(8) Trafficking in persons is increasingly perpetrated by organized, sophisticated criminal enterprises. Such trafficking is the fastest growing source of profits for organized criminal enterprises worldwide. Profits from the trafficking industry contribute to the expansion of organized crime in the United States and worldwide. Trafficking in persons is often aided by official corruption in countries of origin, transit, and destination, thereby threatening the rule of law.

(9) Trafficking includes all the elements of the crime of forcible rape when it involves the involuntary participation of another person in sex acts by means of fraud, force, or coercion.

(10) Trafficking also involves violations of other laws, including labor and immigration codes and laws against kidnapping, slavery, false imprisonment, assault, battery, pandering, fraud, and extortion.

(11) Trafficking exposes victims to serious health risks. Women and children trafficked in the sex industry are exposed to deadly diseases, including HIV and AIDS. Trafficking victims are sometimes worked or physically brutalized to death.

(12) Trafficking in persons substantially affects interstate and foreign commerce. Trafficking for such purposes as involuntary servitude, peonage, and other forms of forced labor has an impact on the nationwide employment network and labor market. Within the context of slavery, servitude, and labor or services which are obtained or maintained through coercive conduct that amounts to a condition of servitude, victims are subjected to a range of violations.

(13) Involuntary servitude statutes are intended to reach cases in which persons are held in a condition of servitude through nonviolent coercion [...]

(14) Existing legislation and law enforcement in the United States and other countries are inadequate to deter trafficking and bring traffickers to justice, failing to reflect the gravity of the offenses involved. No comprehensive law exists in the United States that penalizes the range of offenses involved in the trafficking scheme. Instead, even the most brutal instances of trafficking in the sex industry are often punished under laws that also apply to lesser offenses, so that traffickers typically escape deserved punishment.

(15) In the United States, the seriousness of this crime and its components is not reflected in current sentencing guidelines, resulting in weak penalties for convicted traffickers.

(16) In some countries, enforcement against traffickers is also hindered by official indifference, by corruption, and sometimes even by official participation in trafficking.

(17) Because victims are often illegal immigrants in the destination country, they are repeatedly punished more harshly than the traffickers themselves.

(18) Additionally, adequate services and facilities do not exist to meet victims' needs regarding health care, housing, education, and legal assistance, which safely reintegrate trafficking victims into their home countries.

(19) Victims of severe forms of trafficking should not be inappropriately incarcerated, fined, or otherwise penalized solely for unlawful acts committed as a direct result of being trafficked, such as using false documents, entering the country without documentation, or working without documentation.

(20) Because victims of trafficking are frequently unfamiliar with the laws, cultures, and languages of the countries into which they have been trafficked, because they are often subjected to coercion and intimidation including physical detention and debt bondage, and because they often fear retribution and forcible removal to countries in which they will face retribution or other hardship, these victims often find it difficult or impossible to report the crimes committed against them or to assist in the investigation and prosecution of such crimes.

(21) Trafficking of persons is an evil requiring concerted and vigorous action by countries of origin, transit or destination, and by international organizations.

(22) One of the founding documents of the United States, the Declaration of Independence, recognizes the inherent dignity and worth of all people. It states that all men are created equal and that they are endowed by their Creator with certain unalienable rights. The right to be free from slavery and involuntary servitude is among those unalienable rights. Acknowledging this fact, the United States outlawed slavery and involuntary servitude in 1865, recognizing them as evil institutions that must be abolished. Current practices of sexual slavery and trafficking of women and children are similarly abhorrent to the principles upon which the United States was founded.

(23) The United States and the international community agree that trafficking in persons involves grave violations of human rights and is a matter of pressing international concern. The international community has repeatedly condemned slavery and

involuntary servitude, violence against women, and other elements of trafficking [...]

(24) Trafficking in persons is a transnational crime with national implications. To deter international trafficking and bring its perpetrators to justice, nations including the United States must recognize that trafficking is a serious offense. This is done by prescribing appropriate punishment, giving priority to the prosecution of trafficking offenses, and protecting rather than punishing the victims of such offenses. The United States must work bilaterally and multilaterally to abolish the trafficking industry by taking steps to promote cooperation among countries linked together by international trafficking routes. The United States must also urge the international community to take strong action in multilateral fora to engage recalcitrant countries in serious and sustained efforts to eliminate trafficking and protect trafficking victims. [...]

SEC. 106. Prevention of Trafficking

(a) The President shall establish and carry out international initiatives to enhance economic opportunity for potential victims of trafficking as a method to deter trafficking. Such initiatives may include —

(1) microcredit lending programs, training in business development, skills training, and job counseling;

(2) programs to promote women's participation in economic decision-making;

(3) programs to keep children, especially girls, in elementary and secondary schools, and to educate persons who have been victims of trafficking;

(4) development of educational curricula regarding the dangers of trafficking; and

(5) grants to nongovernmental organizations to accelerate and advance the political, economic, social, and educational roles and capacities of women in their countries.

(b) The President, acting through the Secretary of Labor, the

Secretary of Health and Human Services, the Attorney General, and the Secretary of State, shall establish and carry out programs to increase public awareness, particularly among potential victims of trafficking, of the dangers of trafficking and the protections that are available for victims of trafficking.

(c) The President shall consult with appropriate nongovernmental organizations with respect to the establishment and conduct of initiatives described in subsections (a) and (b).

SEC. 107. Protection and Assistance for Victims of Trafficking

(a) Assistance for victims in other countries.

(1) The Secretary of State and the Administrator of the United States Agency for International Development, in consultation with appropriate nongovernmental organizations, shall establish and carry out programs and initiatives in foreign countries to assist in the safe integration, reintegration, or resettlement, as appropriate, of victims of trafficking. Such programs and initiatives shall be designed to meet the appropriate assistance needs of such persons and their children, as identified by the Task Force.

(2) In establishing and conducting programs and initiatives described in paragraph (1), the Secretary of State and the Administrator of the United States Agency for International Development shall take all appropriate steps to enhance cooperative efforts among foreign countries, including countries of origin of victims of trafficking, to assist in the integration, reintegration, or resettlement, as appropriate, of victims of trafficking, including stateless victims.

(b) Victims in the United States.

(1) Assistance.

(a) Eligibility for benefits and services. Notwithstanding title IV of the Personal Responsibility and Work Opportunity Reconciliation Act of 1996, an alien who is a victim of a severe form of trafficking in persons shall be eligible for benefits and services under any Federal or State program or activity funded or administered by any official or agency described in subparagraph (B) to the same extent as an alien who is admitted to the United States as a refugee under section 207 of the Immigration and Nationality Act.

(b) Requirement to expand benefits and services. Subject to subparagraph (C) and, in the case of nonentitlement programs, to the availability of appropriations, the Secretary of Health and Human Services, the Secretary of Labor, the Board of Directors of the Legal Services Corporation, and the heads of other Federal agencies shall expand benefits and services to victims of severe forms of trafficking in persons in the United States, without regard to the immigration status of such victims.

Appendix C: anti-slavery organizations

The two leading global anti-slavery organizations are: *Anti-Slavery International* (www.antislavery.org), in the UK, and *Free the Slaves* (www.freetheslaves.net), in the US. There are also a number of regional and local organizations that fight slavery and human trafficking:

Anti-Slavery Project of Australia www.antislavery.org.au
Association of Albanian Girls and Women www.aagw.org
Astra Anti Trafficking Action www.astra.org.yu
Bonded Labor Liberation Front www.swamiagnivesh.com
Break the Chain Campaign www.ips-dc.org/campaign/index.htm
Canadian Aid for Southern Sudan www.web.net/cass
Child Labor Coalition www.stopchildlabor.org
Child Rights Information Network www.crin.org
Coalition of Immokalee Workers www.ciw-online.org
Coalition to Abolish Slavery and Trafficking www.trafficked-women.org
Coalition to Stop the Use of Child Soldiers www.child-soldiers.org
Committee Against Modern Slavery www.ccem-anti-slavery.org
Dutch Foundation Against Trafficking in Women www.bayswan.org/FoundTraf.html
ECPAT International www.ecpat.org
Faith Alliance Against Slavery and Trafficking www.faastinternational.org

Global Alliance Against Trafficking in Women www.inet.co.th/org/
gaatw
Global March Against Child Labor http://globalmarch.org
Human Rights Watch www.hrw.org
The Initiative to Stop Human Trafficking www.hks.harvard.edu/cchrp/
isht
International Needs – Ghana www.africaexpress.com/
internationalneedsghana
La Strada www.lastrada.org.ua/?lng=en
Maiti Nepal www.maitinepal.org
Physicians for Human Rights http://physiciansforhumanrights.org
Polaris Project www.polarisproject.org
Protection Project www.protectionproject.org
Rescue and Restore Victims of Human Trafficking www.acf.hhs.gov/
trafficking
Restavec Foundation www.restavec.org
Rugmark Foundation www.rugmark.org
SOS Slaves www.sosesclaves.org

Index

Page numbers in *italics* refer to items in boxes